THE
BOOK OF
CORNWOOD
AND LUTTON

DEVON BOOKS

First published in Great Britain by Devon Books, 1997

ISBN 0 86114 919 X

Cataloguing in Publication Data

CIP record for this title is available from the British Library

DEVON BOOKS

OFFICIAL PUBLISHER TO DEVON COUNTY COUNCIL

In association with

HALSGROVE

PUBLISHING, MEDIA AND DISTRIBUTION
Halsgrove House
Lower Moor Way
Tiverton
Devon EX16 6SS

Tel: 01882 243242
Fax: 01884 243325

DEDICATION
**This book is dedicated to the
people of the Parish,
past and present**

Printed in Great Britain by Bookcraft Ltd, Somerset.

Contents

Acknowledgements

This book would not have been possible without the help, enthusiasm and support given by the inhabitants of Cornwood Parish, those of today and yesterday. Special thanks must be given to those who have lent photographs and memorabilia, and remembered how things were years ago:

Mary Abbott; Blanche Andrew; Ethel Andrew; Rosalind Andrew; Kath Andrews; Margaret Atkins: Margaret Baker: Ann Baldacchino: Dave Barker: Doris and Harry Baskerville; Shelley Bastone; Linda Bennett; Marion Blackshaw; Norah Blackshaw; Muriel Bloomfield; Dave Brewer; Jack Bradley; Sheila Brown; Margaret and Charles Bullock; Vi Burden; Jane Burden; Auriol Butler; Elsie Cannon; Edna Carleton; John Rose-Casemore; Richard Rose-Casemore; Sue Cousins; Clifford Cox; Barbara Devine: Gary Devine; Pat den Hollander; Lynn Diffey; Anita Donne: Douglas Drew; Rosemary Elsworth; Lilian and David Farnham; Edna German; Mrs Glen-Leary; Dorothy Glover: Molly Godfrey: Marjorie Goodman: Barbara Green; Luthfi Gulliver; Elsie Handford; Charles Hankin: Nancy Hare: Helen Harris: Eleanor Haynes; Ida Hopper: Tina Horton; Phillip Hurn; Ivy James: Olive Jeffery; Peter Johnson and colleagues at W.B.B.; Alison Jonas; Wyn Jonas; Pam Keane; Minnie Kingdom; Daisy Kingwell; John Lennard of Plymouth Art Centre; Eileen Luscombe; Kit and Paul Manning; Ivor Martin; Mercy Matthews; Nigel Matthews; Barbara and Tony Mills; Eva and John Moysey; Rachel Mudge; Lewis John Munford; Hilary Newcombe; Joyce Nicholson; William Norrish; Janet and John Northmore: Marianne and Peter Odling-Smee; Phil Page of English Nature; Mrs Robert Parker; Doris Pengelley; Eric Phillips: Richard Phillips: Verity Phillips; May Poynter; Sue Pritchard-Jenkins; Paul Rendell; Frances Rendle; Joyce Rendle; Mildred Rendle; Elayne Rouse; Terry Ryder; Paul Salmon; Betty and Reg Sampson; Ann and Peter Sandover; Herbert Sharp; Margaret and Peter Short; Phyllis Short; Sydney Short; Barbara Simpson; Clifford Small; Reg Steer; Muriel and Basil Stephens; Dave Turner; Kathleen Wakeham: Liz Warley; Mary West; Fred Willcocks; Furnley Willcocks; Veryan Williams-Wynn; Graham Woodliffe; Hilda and Andrew Wotton; Richard Wotton;

I am most grateful to Geoff Cook; Gavin Dollard: David Edwards; Sally Fairman; Judith and Keith Farmer; Bert Ford: Don McDonald: Terry Morrison; John Northey; Marilyn Sharp; Edith Skelley; Bert Small: Marilyn Small; Tom Squires; Barbara Thomas: Sue Warry: and Freddy Woodward who not only provided photographs but also helped me write the text and last but not least especial thanks to my husband, Eric, who has written, compiled, and used his camera wherever required, and helped cope with many piles of paper.

Meriel Dobinson, Stone, Cornwood.
November 1997

Foreword

by The Earl of Morley
HM Lord Lieutenant for Devon

Most villages originated as small, isolated, independent rural communities, whose members not only lived, but worked in the immediate area and which very much generated their own community life and spirit from their own resources. Such were Cornwood and Lutton, which both figure in the Domesday Book.

These communities were not always havens of peace as there would be quarrels, jealousies and rivalries, such as are portrayed in many classic novels. But with the passage of time and evolution of transport much has changed. Communities are no longer self-sufficient. People can travel and commute to work and many outside influences have been brought to bear. In this process much individuality has often been lost.

The people of Cornwood and Lutton are therefore to be congratulated on regenerating a strong community spirit as demonstrated in this book.

I hope that all who read it will recognise the hard work and dedication which has gone into it and all the benefits which will accrue to the community, and that it will be an example to others.

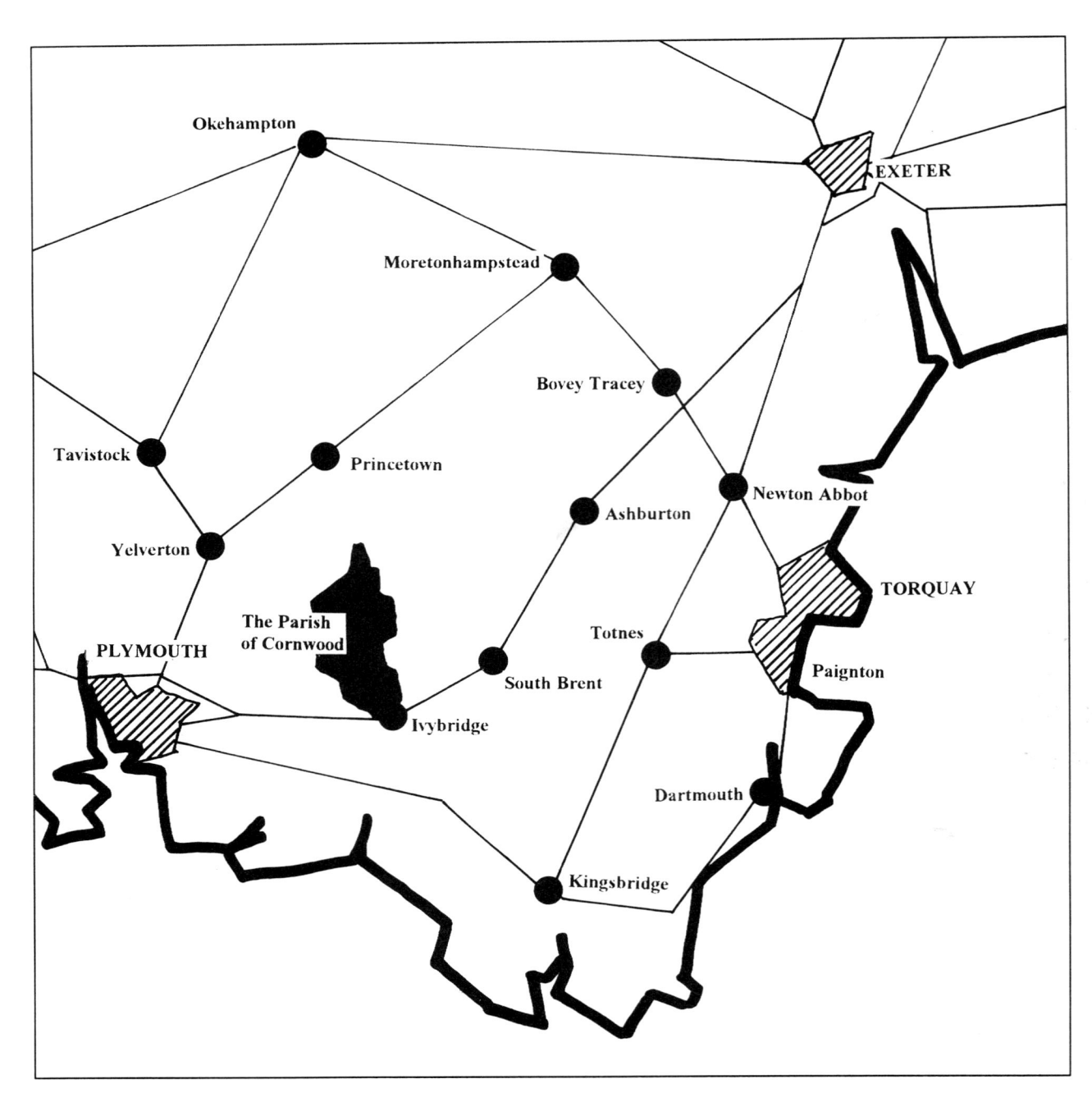

Cornwood in the South Hams

Introduction

The Parish of Cornwood, with a present population of just over one thousand, includes the two villages of Cornwood and Lutton. Generally regarded as a 'Dartmoor Parish' six thousand of its ten thousand acres are moorland. The boundary of Dartmoor National Park takes in Cornwood Village, but not Lutton, and to the south is the fast-growing town of Ivybridge. The river Yealm runs down through the middle of the parish.

In August 1996, in a marquee at the Cornwood Agricultural Show, the Lord Lieutenant of Devon, Lord Morley, unveiled the Parish Map of Cornwood. This beautiful and artistic representation of the parish, showing some of its buildings, flora, fauna and landmarks, was the result of months of work. It prompted many residents, and those with local knowledge, to talk about their memories of past events, backed up with photographs, newspaper cuttings, scrapbooks and memorabilia.

Whenever a display of photographs of some of the older properties in the village, now greatly altered, was held, it would prompt a stream of memories of previous years. Very often names would be given to the faces portrayed from a bygone age.

All this, the history of our community over the last centuries, is far too valuable to lose. Therefore the gathering together of our past, much of it pictorial, in the form of a book is a very good way of celebrating the end of this century.

Cornwood Show - 17 August 1996. Left to right - back row: *Gavin Dollard, Lady Morley, Meriel Dobinson, Lord Morley, Sally Fairman, Sue Warry, Jim Estcourt* (extreme right). Front row: *Eric Dobinson, John Northey, Keith Farmer, Barbara Thomas.*

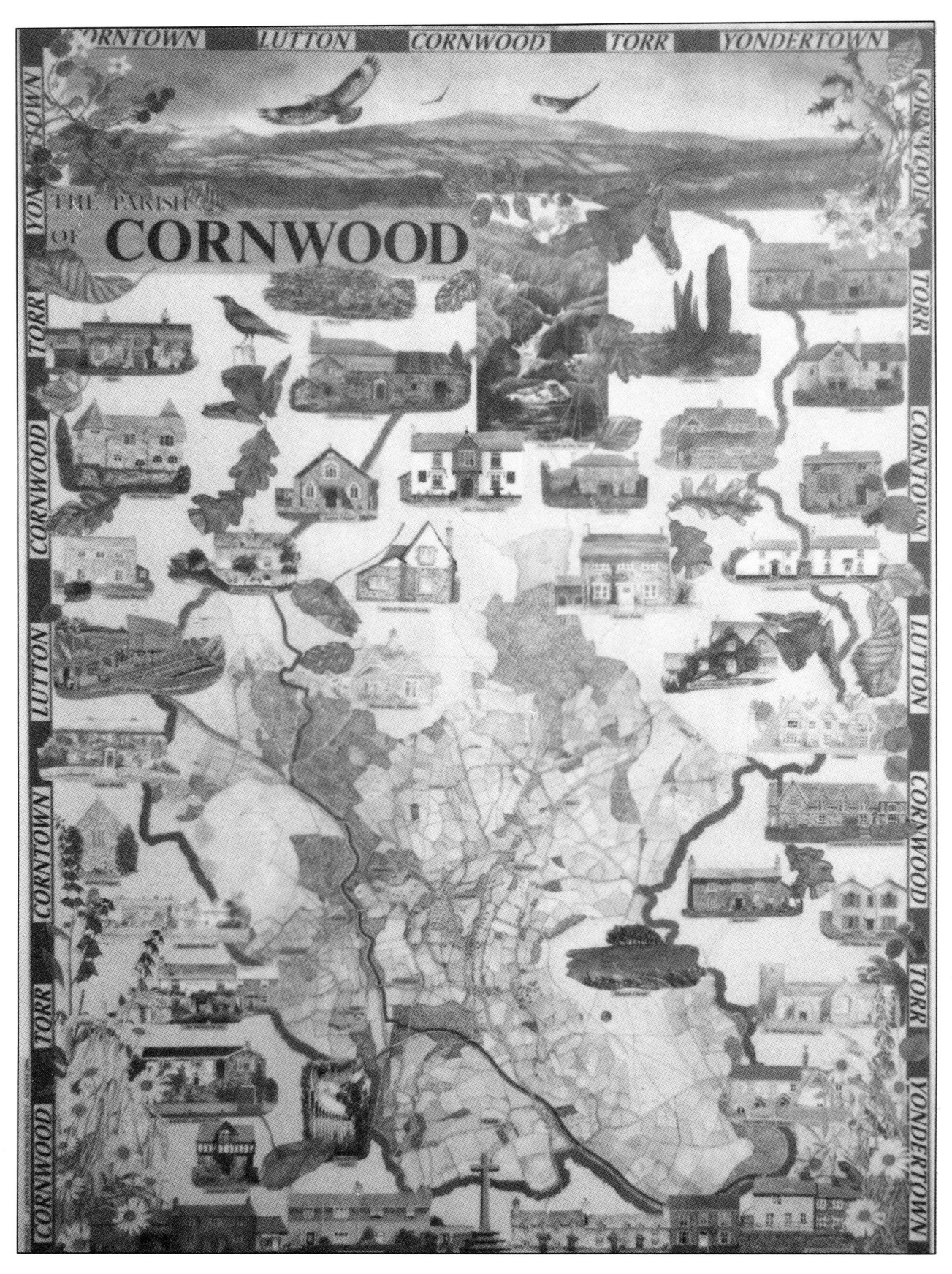

The Cornwood Parish Map.

Cornwood Within the National Park

Dartmoor can be many things to many people. Some will associate it with the convict prison, Uncle Tom Cobley, the Hound of the Baskervilles, pixies, ponies, a pleasant drive out on a Sunday afternoon to Dartmeet for a cream tea. To others, looking for peace and solitude, it offers an unspoiled wilderness, an oasis where for a few hours one can escape the pressures, traffic and pollution of modern life. It is also the home and workplace of many living within the boundary of the National Park.

The eleven National Parks in England and Wales were born out of the post-war vision of those people who wished to ensure that the best of our countryside should be identified and protected and that public access for recreation be secured.

John Dower, an architect, was asked by the government to prepare a report on how the concept of National Parks in other countries could be adopted for England and Wales. His report was published in 1945 and its recommendations accepted. This led to the 1949 National Parks and Access to the Countryside Act, and Cornwood (or most of it) became part of the fourth National Park in 1951.

The statutory objectives of the National Park Authorities are to conserve and enhance the quality of the landscape and to promote public enjoyment of that landscape. This is a difficult balancing act, protecting the natural beauty of the Park while considering the interests of agriculture, tourism, military use, forestry, water extraction, mineral working etc. Inevitably there will be conflicts of interests and compromises sometimes have to be made.

It would be fair to say that the parish of Cornwood represents all those qualities which originally made Dartmoor worthy of the designation National Park. This is best illustrated by following the river Yealm from its humble beginning high on the southern plateau as it issues from the blanket bog near Langcombe Hill and swiftly descends through granite boulder strewn heather moorland, cascading down the spectacular waterfall at Yealm Steps, growing wider and moving more slowly through the ancient oak and beech of Dendles Wood Nature Reserve before emerging into a typical Devonshire farmed landscape, finally passing below Cornwood village and leaving

The National Park boundary sign, approaching Cornwood, just north of Moor Cross.

the National Park behind at Blachford Viaduct. We will see that as well as flowing through virtually every type of Dartmoor habitat, the river witnesses testimony to man's occupation of Cornwood parish from the 4000 year old cists, cairns, stone rows and hut circles through mediaeval longhouses, 14th century blowing houses (used for smelting tin) and on to the more recent past of the corn mill at Wisdom and the beautiful structure carrying the Great Western Railway over the river Valley.

Of the 10 000 acres within the parish, 6000 are moorland and woodland - this partly explains the reason why it is unaffected by mass tourism but does offer wonderful opportunities for those interested in quiet recreational pursuits such as walking, horse riding and observing the superb variety of flora and fauna present in the area. National Park status should ensure that this situation will remain unchanged for the foreseeable future.

**Paul Salmon, Senior Ranger,
Dartmoor National Park.**

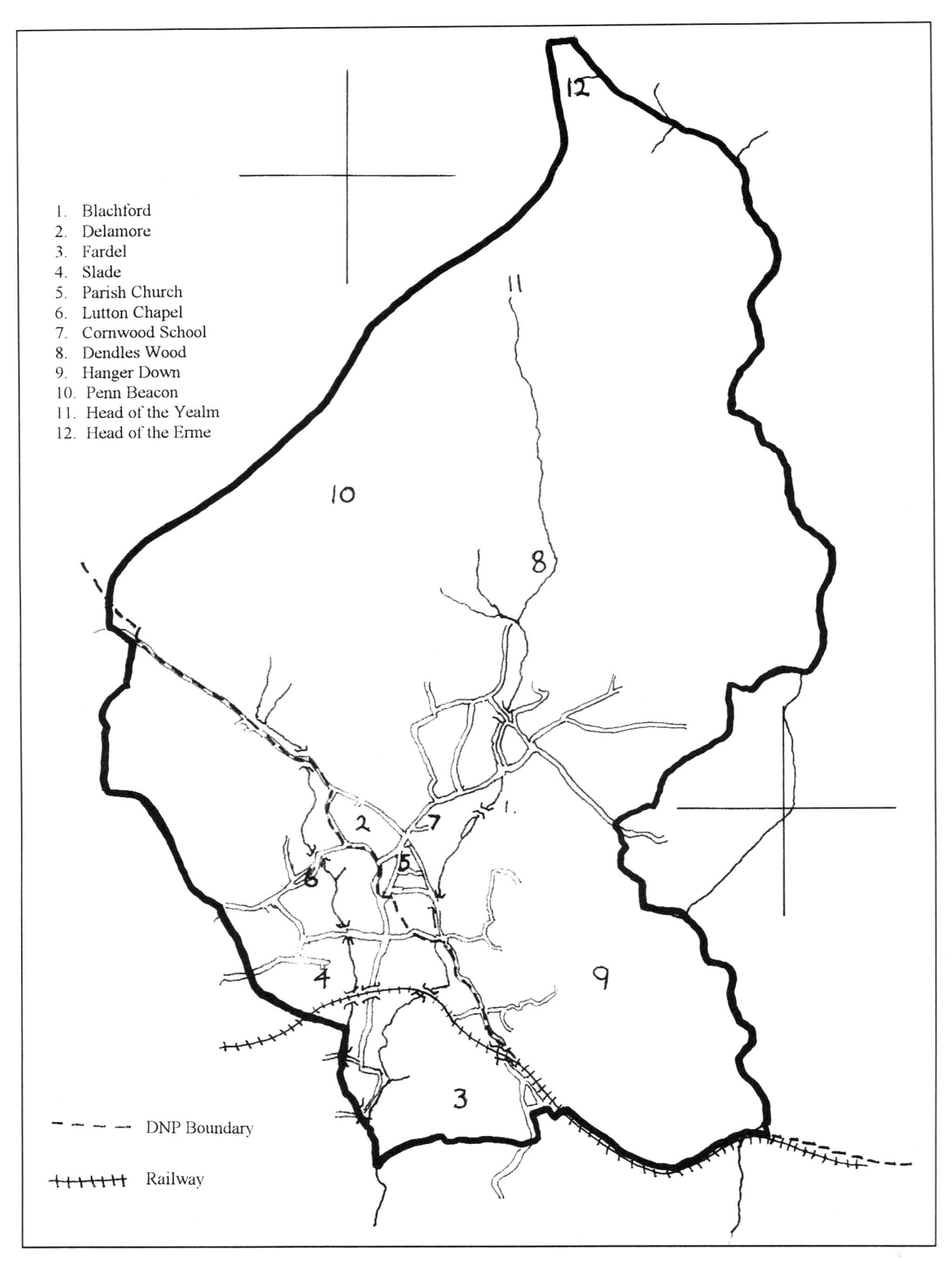

1. Blachford
2. Delamore
3. Fardel
4. Slade
5. Parish Church
6. Lutton Chapel
7. Cornwood School
8. Dendles Wood
9. Hanger Down
10. Penn Beacon
11. Head of the Yealm
12. Head of the Erme

– – – – DNP Boundary

++++++ Railway

The Parish of Cornwood

The Parish Bounds - Boxing the Compass

To 'Box the Compass', says the dictionary, is 'to rehearse the points of the compass in correct order'. So on one of those beautiful clear days, let us look North to Penn Beacon where at this distance the grazing animals are small, slowly moving objects on the slopes now green after so much rain, but warmly lit by the sun shining on areas of russet bracken.

Moving East, the horizon distances, and then becomes more broken as we see the Yealm Steps, and, even at this distance, the sparkle of tumbling water. By now the open moor has given way to woodlands on the lower slopes, giving a great variety of colour, from the dark conifers of the plantation to the areas of oak and beech - part of which is Dendles National Nature Reserve. Then across and up the valley, less densely wooded: on Eastwards to the next valley - the Erme valley. At this distance the valley slopes look so soft but one knows they are really very stony. Not many trees here, but down in the fold of the hill the tip of the primeval forest, Piles Copse, is just visible. On the horizon, above the faint line which is the old tramway to the abandoned clay pits, is Three Barrows, where, on rare occasions of celebration, a beacon fire might still be lit.

Our compass taking us through the East, we look down a little to Wilkey's Moor, again beautiful woods clothe the lower acres, carrying the eye up to Western Beacon and Butterdon Hill and then down, and on to a shining segment of a circle reflecting the sunshine - dazzling gold of sun on sea - the eye travels through South and West of South, to Cornwall. In between our escarpment and the far horizon of Cornwall one can recognise familiar landmarks of Plymouth, and, dropping the eyes, the whole of South Hams: then looking up again following the compass point West and North West, also West of North, the moon-like landscape of china clay workings, with Cornwood and its church seeming to lie at its very foot. The church - St Michael and All Angels - stands out very strongly.

Where then is this unique foothill of the Moor on whose ancient springy turf we are standing? From where can we box the compass and feast the eyes on such a varied, beautiful and completely unspoilt panorama? Hanger Down, of course. There on the South-West facing slope is The Hanger, a landmark for many miles.

All this within easy reach of Cornwood: the public bridleway running - a lovely broad green ride - from Hall Cross to Whingreen (or vice-versa). Hanger Down is part of Dartmoor National Park and like all land in the National Park is privately owned, so enjoyment of this unspoiled downland is dependent on the good will of the owner.

Mrs Kathleen Nightingale.

A distant view of Cornwood with the china clay workings beyond.

Boundary Markers

Left: The boundary stone at Langcombe Head; BB = Blachford Bound. Top: Broad Rock, northernmost point of the parish, on the Abbot's Way. Above: Hillson's House, Stall Moor.

The northern boundary wall; High House Waste and Dendles Waste.

Beating the Bounds

At 7.30 hours, Saturday 10th September, 1981 sixteen members of Cornwood Church gathered on Slade Lawn for inspection by walk-leader Len Copley. Seven ladies and nine men in various items of waterproof clothing and generally adequately booted were found 'fit-for-service'. With the Vicar in the lead we set off at a brisk pace along Slade drive to tackle the twenty-two miles of the parish boundary.

Stert Bridge to Little Stert and the rhythm was being established, along the footpath to Marks Bridge, Cadleigh Lodge, Stibb and Langham. Up Langham Hill and on to Henlake Down with two of our ladies breaking the trail which led across the back of Hanger to Hall Cross. Here it was decided to make a brief halt.

'Gird up your loins', and on again to New Waste Reservoir. Now 'Sir' took a lead and it was certainly not weariness making the pace seem quicker. The taunt of 'keep up, the geriatrics' spurred us on although the grouping was less compact as we reached the west bank of the Erme. Why did the weather forecast have to prove correct as we moved deeper into the Moor? Rain was falling steadily as we passed briefly the Beehive Hut - that interesting feature where tinners on the Erme once left their tools overnight. Nine miles behind us and we were following the Stone Row for almost a mile of its two and a quarter mile length and we swung nor'-westward to the most northerly point of the parish - Broad Rock on the Abbots Way. Sir had said, 'Lunch at Broad Rock', and so it had to be in spite of howling wind and pelting rain which soggied the sandwiches and sadly diluted coffee.

Once more, only encouraged by the thought that we were homeward bound with only eleven miles to go! Over Langcombe Head and the weather getting even worse as we struggled towards Shell Top. Then the long walk down through Dendles Wood to Higher Hele where most found welcome shelter, although three of the rear-guard staggered past and on to Cornwood! Eventually all reached Slade where, soaking wet yet still in good heart, solace was found in 'a wee dram'.

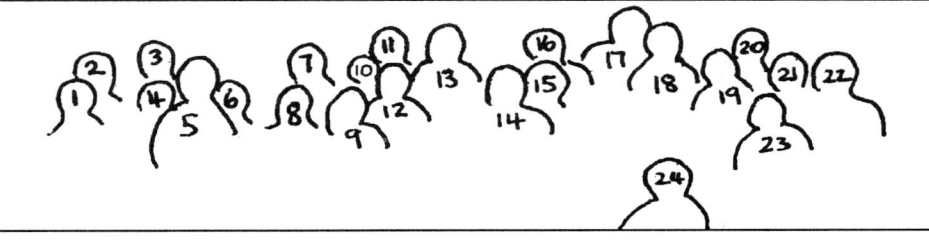

Beating the bounds
8 June, 1991.

1. *Rosemary Edwards.*
2. *Keith Barsby.*
3. *Derek Butler.*
4. *Monica Barsby.*
5. *Paul Rendell.*
7. *Donald Bayley.*
8. *Sheila Williams.*
9. *Clare Williams.*
10. *Jenny Bayley.*
12. *Tony Williams.*
13. *Tom Squires.*
14. *Richard Roberts.*
15. *John Roberts.*
16. *John Northmore.*
17. *Rev. John Perry.*
18. *Len Copley.*
19. *Karyn Yarnold.*
20. *David Farnham.*
21. *Molly Godfrey.*
22. *Audrey Perfitt.*
23. *Sue Warry.*
24. *Richard Yarnold.*

Hawns and Dendles - The 'In Between'

This area of the parish could easily be called the 'in-between', as it lies between Stalldown Barrow to the east, Penn Beacon to the west, to true high moorland of Dartmoor to the north and the lush fields of the farming areas of Coombe, Higher Hele and Lower Hele to the south. This is an area of outstanding interest and beauty.

It can best be visualised as a letter Y with the left hand arm being a valley between Hawns Wood and High House Waste, with the stream known as Broadall Lake. The right hand arm of the Y is a valley carrying the river Yealm through Dendles Wood. In between these two arms is a spur of high land rising to nearly 1000 feet. This is visible from the surrounding moorland, and also from the village of Cornwood. It was planted with conifers in the 1950s and these were felled during the summers of '95 and '96.

Dendles Wood has since 1965 been a National Nature Reserve, owned and managed by English Nature. Through the middle of it cascades the river Yealm. Oak and beech trees dominate, and in the southerly part, known as Fernfires Wood, there are many beeches over 300 years old.

Rainfall in the whole area is very high, up to 75 inches per year, giving rise to very lush, moist conditions, where ferns and mosses of infinite variety grow in profusion. Birds that breed in this landscape include the buzzard, great spotted woodpecker, grey wagtail, redstart, wood warbler, pied flycatcher and nuthatch. Red and fallow deer have been observed, and of particular interest to the biologist was the discovery, in the 1980s, of the blue ground beetle. This beetle was thought to be extinct in Britain. It is a globally threatened species.

The woodland area to the west, running up from Dendles Green towards High House Waste and Hawns Wood, either side of Broadall Lake is similar, though with rather more varied types of trees. These are mainly oak and beech, with hazel, rowan and willow. This area, and the spur of higher ground in the middle, was purchased by Dartmoor National Park Authority in 1997, and they are preparing long-term plans to return it to its natural state through good management.

This 'in-between' land of Cornwood Parish is rich in archaeological history. There is a Bronze Age cairn circle with a cist, two Bronze Age settlements containing at least nineteen hut circles, with associated walling, whilst the outer boundary is built on to a long prehistoric reave, or low

Picnic at Dendles Wood, about 1912. Left to right: *Miss Laura Crimp (George Crimp's sister); Ida Griffiths (niece of Mrs Crimp); Governess at Blachford; Mrs Mary Crimp (George Crimp's first wife); Mrs Emily Greep.*

boundary wall, which continues in a straight line to Penn Beacon. There are also two medieval farmsteads, possibly longhouses, with associated fields standing inside a fine example of a cornditch wall.

The question of how this beautiful area got its name has been open to debate for many years, though the theory that holds most support is that the name is based on two people who at one time owned the land. A lady named Hawns has not as yet been confirmed, though there is ample proof of the existence of a Mr Daniels, whose name could easily be corrupted into Dendles of today.

Hawns and Dendles has been popular with visitors as far back as the closing years of the last century when commercially produced postcards were available. It was found that some refreshment was also desirable, and the result of this was the rustic tea gardens on the banks of the Yealm at Yeo, and cream teas to be found at Coombe. Today one would need to return to the village to visit the Post Office Tea Rooms.

A true spirit of the Edwardian age, Dr Fox of Plymouth, who loved Hawns and Dendles, obtained permission from the owners to create a garden of his own in the moist and cool conditions of Hawns Wood. He planted exotic species including, it is said, rhododendrons brought back from plant-finding expeditions to the Himalayas, and many varieties of ferns. He built a small shelter, and invited friends to picnic there.

Dr Fox arranged for Mr Stacey, who owned one of the first three automobiles in the village, to taxi him from the railway station to the end of the track north of Higher Hele. From there he and his friends continued on foot to the garden. Some of the trees and shrubs he planted remain to this day and it is proposed to retain and maintain this unique woodland garden.

Septimus Green, much respected and revered Victorian headmaster of Cornwood School, also admired the beauty and wonder of Hawns and Dendles. He expressed these feelings in one of his poems, which in 1897 was included in the book of poems *Jennifred* dedicated to Horatio Tennyson, brother of Alfred Lord Tennyson, three verses of which follow:

Hawns and Dendles, 1890.

From Troubles far of fretful trade,
For mortals wearied with the strife
Of the loud city's feverish life,
Green waits a wild glen's gladdening glade.

By lanes of feathery ferns embanked,
With many a winding runs the way
With sweet-breath'd primrose golden-gay,
Or with proud foxgloves richly pranked.

Till sudden lo! beneath our feet,
With welcome to its native wood
The yeasty Yealm her amber floods,
Rolls Blachford-ward with music sweet.

Unfortunately there is no public access to this most beautiful part of the parish without written permission from the Nature Conservancy Council, as private land has to be crossed before entry.

Cairn circle and cist, Dendles Waste. Cists are stone 'coffins' containing interments and on Dartmoor are often associated with stone rows.

The stone row on Stall Moor. The purpose of such rows is unknown. They are linked to known prehistoric settlements, often associated with cemeteries.

The Fardel Stone. For whatever reasons, prehistoric moorland settlements were abandoned, but perhaps continued at lower levels. The Roman period seems to have by-passed the parish. The Fardel Stone with its Ogham inscriptions is dated to between the sixth and eighth centuries. Standing nearly six feet high, it was found across the stream called the Fardel Brook and was later to be used as a ring post in a shed in the yard of Fardel Manor House. Captain Pode presented the stone to the British Museum in 1861. The Ogham and loosely similar Latin texts provide evidence, along with other examples from Devon, of Irish settlers in Western Britain. Reproduced with the kind permission of the British Museum.

Early History

Within the area now recognised as Cornwood parish, both archaeological and written evidence suggest that people have lived here for a very long time. The upland part of the parish, still grazed by animals whose farming owners have such rights on the moor, contain many antiquities dated to the Bronze Age, from about 2000 years BC. There are circular house foundations, walled enclosures, many to be seen below Penn Beacon, and on the slopes of Stall Moor, and along the banks of the River Erme , the eastern boundary of the present parish. These are typical of prehistoric remains found all over Dartmoor, and since tin is required to make bronze, it may be that there was early exploitation of the tin deposits here.

Ritual cists and cairns associated with burial rites may also be seen on higher ground, perhaps above what was cultivatable land, and much stone may have been re-used in later times for gateposts and troughs and in walls. More enigmatic are the stone rows, one lost at Cholwichtown, but a very fine one survives on Stall Moor.

The Domesday survey of 1086, at the instigation of William I, shows there was settlement throughout the parish, though the roots of the population are difficult to ascertain. The manor was an organised unit in place before the advent of the present parish, and five were recorded. They belonged to Edmaer of Curnwood, Dunne of Dunintone and Ferdendelle, and Aluuin of over and nether Blachevrde. These Saxon lords would probably have attended the Moot or meeting for the Hundred of Ermington whose settlements lay between the Avon and the Yealm, bounded by Plympton Hundred to the west and Stanborough Hundred to the east.

William rewarded his knights with land, and this area was no exception. Cornwood, Fardel and Dinnaton were held in fee by a knight Reginald, from Robert Count of Mortain, the half-brother of William himself. In a later book of fees, 'Curnwod and Ludeton' are held from William de Ferrers, and later again 'Lutton or Lyneton' by Ralph Bryt.

Besides the '3 unbroken mares' or Dartmoor ponies (so often quoted about Cornwood in Domesday), there was meadow, pasture, woodland and stock all to be valued, along with the villeins. Dinnaton and Fardel manors had four and five farmers (*villani*) respectively. Cornwood had eight *villani*, and if each had the 'hide' area of 60 to 120 acres, it was thought they would have sufficient to support a family, extended to three generations. Added to these were nineteen 'borders' or smallholders, giving a total of 44 heads of families, just one short of the total as listed paying the Lay Subsidy Tax of 1332.

The Devonshire Lay Subsidy (a tax list) of 1332 places named people within the parish area at specific places, and listed still under the two manors of Fardel and Cornwood. Wealth is indicated by contributions, the most by Peter de Ralegh at Fardel of 5 shillings. Both William de Dynington and Walter de Shirewill pay 2s, while Walter at More (Moor Cross) pays 18d, John at Parke and Walter at Tornwodaton (Corntown?) pay 16d each, Robert de Yeodesworthi and John de Blachesworthi half that at 8d each. Lesser contributions come from John at Sturte, Joan at Slade and John at Torr. Robert Gibbe who is listed also in the Stannary Rolls of the period with Richard Gibbe would imply tin-mining interests between 1327 and 1349.

The medieval period has left evidence on the ground as well. Several small abandoned settlements may be found on the periphery of present day cultivated land at Ford Waste, Ford Bard, High House Waste, Hawns, Harrowthorn and Parkland Newtake.

Some field banks associated with these longhouses may be seen, and others in the present fields at Tin Park. There are the routes of the former and still extant drove-roads to the moor still traceable, though Watery Lane is impassable. At the roadside above Tin Park opposite what was the old entrance to Cholwichtown is a cross with uncertain history, though this road to Tavistock must be ancient. There is also part of a cross used as a gatepost at Hanger.

Cholwichtown farmhouse seems to belong to this early period, and over the next few centuries, as was common elsewhere, there was building and rebuilding at Fardel, Slade, Hanger, Lower Hele and Wisdom Farm as yeomen farmers made their way in the world. It may be that the wool for the prosperous cloth trade, and investments in tin-workings beside the Rivers Erme and Yealm were responsible. Mr J. Pode found a tin ingot buried in a meadow in the Slade valley in 1897 which he presented to the Plymouth Atheneum, but was later lost.

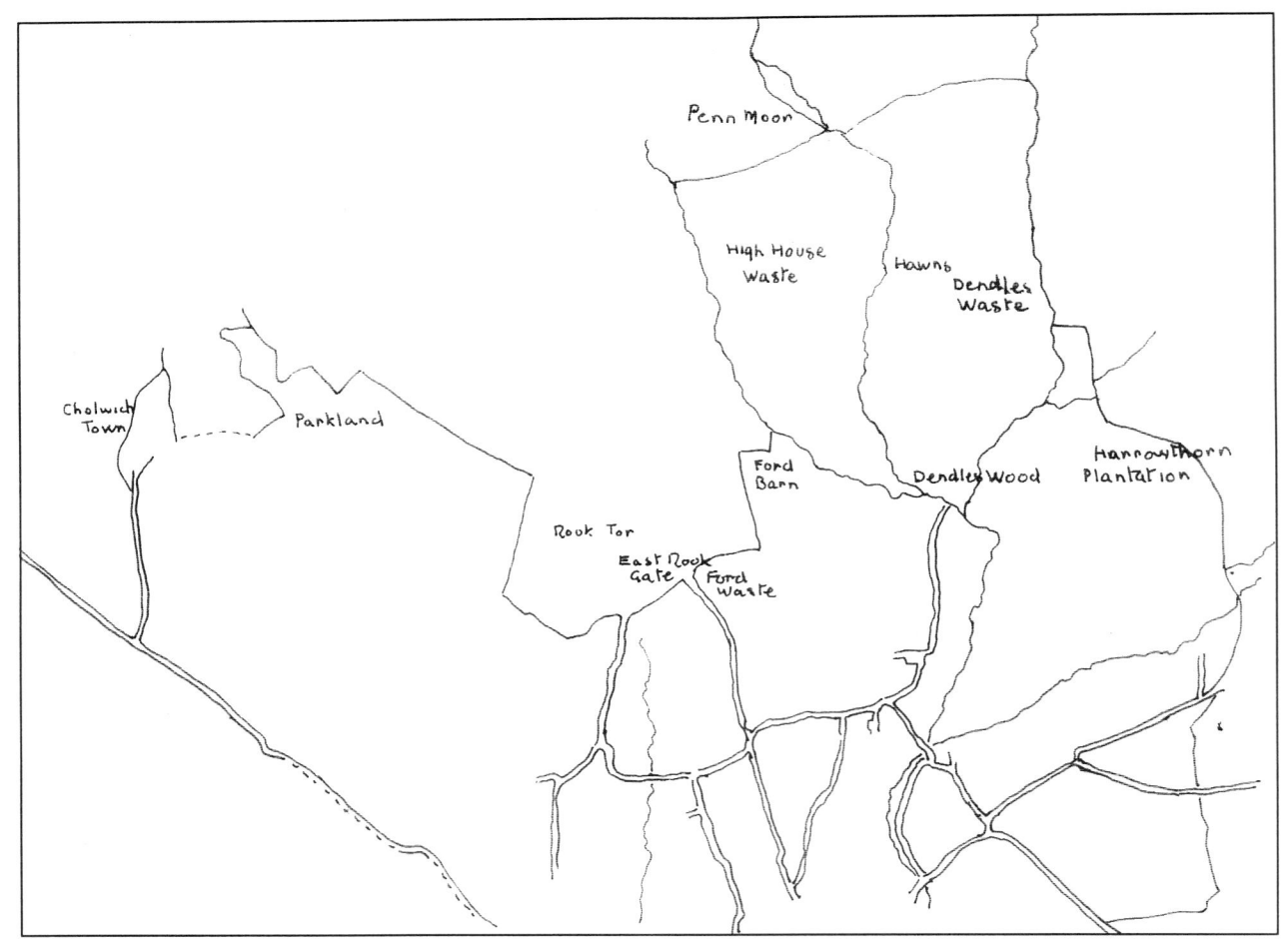

Abandoned settlements on the periphery of present day cultivated land.

Several mills must also have been in use, some are identifiable by name, Wisdom which still has its wheel and leat, and Slade to which present building a leat may be traced from the Yealm. Fardel and Old Park are also mentioned as being in place as late as 1850, and there are Mill fields identified on the Tithe map on the Piall Brook below Lutton Great Meadow.

Documents of the late sixteenth and early seventeenth centuries list many of the inhabitants of the parish. The Devon Subsidy Rolls 1524-7 have 131 one names liable for taxation. In 1524 John Cole of Slade was suspected by the commissioners for the taxation of not declaring the full value of his goods, and having been 'warned by the bayle of the seyd hundred of Ermyngton to appere before the seyd commissioners [at] Kyngs Brygge... made defaute and appered not'. However his contributions (£133) were enormous compared to the rest: the next being Simon Rede at £80 for goods, and William Rede sen. at £30. Joan Hele a widow paid £22 for goods, and Nicholas Hele £18. Simon Hanger paid only £2 for his land, and John Hele £8. Walter Choleswych paid £22 for goods and

John Sherewyll £15. Walter Stertt paid goods value £17. The majority of inhabitants paid taxes in the £5 down to £1 range.

The 1581 Subsidy lists 39 heads of households: 18 taxed by Goods and 21 by Land wealth. Presumably only heads of households were liable for taxation at this time as the 1641 Protestation Returns list 221 names in the parish.

Henry Smith was the vicar at this date, John Browne the Overseer of the Poor, John Lavers and Thomas Browne were constables and Richard Turrin [Turpin?] the churchwarden. All assistance to the poor, law and order, and the state of the roads were parish responsibilities. Other names of the period include: Banded [Bowden?], Greepe, Hannaford, Savery, Symons and Tocher [Tucker?].

The Hearth Tax Returns of 1674 have 298 households, and perhaps are more indicative of the total number of families that might have lived in the village. The lists include familiar names such as Andrew, Baskervill (various spellings), Bowden, Browne, Charels [Charles?], Gardiner, Harris, Maddocke, Mason, Pearse, Sheapherd, Steart, Stevens, Turpin and Wiate. John Rogers

Cross above Tin Park - once saw use as a gatepost.

appears as does William Cholwich described as 'Gent'.

Among the 'poor' are Luccrafte, Mills, Blackler and Towsen. Mrs Penelope Hele pays for 13 hearths, Edmund Foscue (Fortescue) 8 at Hanger, as did Robert Andrewes.

An interesting inventory of 1647 describes the actual possessions of one, George Gripe (Greep) of Cornwood, being also a soldier of the garrison at Plymouth at the time of the Civil War. His belongings at death include '2 kine [cattle] £6, 1 hooge [hog] 4s; 1 crookes [crocks?] 10s; 2 pannes 8s; 2 skillets 4s; 1 tinning candelsticke 8d; 1 washen tubbe 1s; 8 wooden dishes 1 ladle 4d; 1 brandiron 1 gridiron; 2 dustebeeds 3 blankeets 2 coverlets 2 fethered bolsters 3 pillowes £1 14s; 2 chares 1s 6d; 2 olde cheestes 1s; 2 pare of Lummes £1 2s; 1 winding sheete 1s. These goods indicate his farming and weaving interests as well as the chattels of the period which he owned.

During the 17th and 18th centuries , as England prospered in trade and the Empire began to grow, the houses in the parish were extended and improved. These included Blachford, remodelled from the 16th century by the Rogers family, Hanger, Fardel, Higher Hele and Slade. The Parish Registers indicate a steady increase in numbers within the parish by virtue of there being fewer burials than baptisms, especially from the second

half of the 18th century. Sampling every five years shows familiar names appearing, Horton, Mudge, Luscombe, Corber, Northmore, Hilson, Tall, Greep, Mumford, Blackler, Samson, Symons, Ford and Searle.

From 1793, the Rev. Duke Younge included in the registers the occupation of the father of baptised infants, the most common being that of 'husbandman'. Some, referred to specifically as farmers, were tenants of the large farms. Craftsmen can be identified, carpenters were named Horton and Nelder, blacksmiths were Sandover and Mudge, Sanders and Phillips were masons, and Luscombe and Tall were millers. There was a Baskerville in the militia, a marine called Willcocks, a cooper called Furneaux and Mudge the thatcher.

Causes of death were also recorded by this diligent clergyman, from old age (frequently), phthisis, consumption, smallpox; palsy, fever, paralysis, whooping cough, angina and scarlet fever.

The 19th century provides more documentary evidence of the parish and its inhabitants, especially after the census was instituted for every ten years, and families like the Mudges and Sampsons have been able to research their own lineage.

The 1842 Tithe Map and Apportionment book are valuable for the lay-out of the fields and buildings, owners and occupiers at one point in time. The statute measure of lands showed 10 680 cultivated acres, though 7459 are described as commons and must be the moorland grazing. Arable acres total 1852 and meadow and pasture 577 acres. Woods and plantations total 700 acres and there were 92 orchards and gardens.

Sir John Leman Rogers was by far the owner of most land. William Pode at Fardel owned Fardel Mill , Slade and Lower Stert. The Earl of Morley let Cholwichtown to Philip Luscombe and Parkland to John Chapple. Sir John Rogers' tenants included the Horton family, Trobridge at Uppaton and Sherrell, Alexander at Dinnaton and Alexander Jn. at Higher Hele, with Honor at Wilkiemoor. The Hortons seem to have been prolific, 116 of them buried in the churchyard, by far the most of any family.

Sir John Rogers' other tenants included Thomas Walk at Houndle, Henry Mudge at Moor (Cross), Robert Sercombe at Lower Hele and Wisdom, Robert Hilson at Stone, Thomas Searle at Coombe; while Richard Colton farmed Torr and his son Watercombe and Gorage. Henry Sanders farmed Brook and Yadesworthy. These tenancies changed hands through the century and may be traced further through the lists in Kelly's and White's Directories after 1850.

Wisdome Farm: granite mullion with drip mould.

The carved granite doorway at Wisdome

Lutton village shows a different pattern, with individual owners of small plots in their own right. This, together with that of the few surviving long fields, may reflect a more open village, and possibly farming by strips in large open fields in much earlier times. James Doddridge owned Lutton farm and John Luscombe owned property in Yondertown Square, and three cottages behind, as well as Little Uppaton. Henry and James Mudge owned a field or two and cottages. Richard and Mary Roberts lived in a tiny house opposite the present Chapel Sunday School, but also owned 'cottages sheds and gardens'. Josias Nelder also held land as did Arthur Skelly, Jane and James Shepherd. Sampson Shepherd had several properties to let and was the owner of East Rooke and trustee for the Charity land.

In Cornwood William Mackworth Praed owned most of the properties along Bond Street and Fore Street. The Inn was the Tavistock Inn. Robert Mudge had his wheelwright's premises with the yard in front. Richard Shepherd, Robert Elford and Harry Elliot were tenants in the cottages. Charlotte Vivian was at the Old Post Office and three tenants occupied the Old Clergy house. A farm seems to have occupied the site of the present school, with barns and bays opposite, and no doubt the Smithy was a working business.

While the village has seen the number of houses increase during the 20th century, some older houses, presumably rather poor, have disappeared. Thomas King lived in a house below Lutton Farm on what now just remains as a level piece of ground beyond a gateway off the road. The road at Torr followed a slightly different course with several cottages marked and occupied, and no doubt the present ones must have been divided. Three cottages existed and were occupied below the present Waterleat House, then called Waterlee, and along the footpath to Slade Mill some banks within a triangular shape being all that now remains.

After 1850 there were to be many changes in the parish, and many of them can be seen today. The railway with its great viaducts were in place, the New Road in Lutton replaced Chapel Lane as the thoroughfare, and new roads were opened by the side of Oak Park and along the Yealm from Vicarage Bridge to Wisdom Bridge.

The schools in Lutton and Cornwood replaced the Dame School at Churchtown, and the new Delamore House came into being. Many of these changes were to be seen and experienced by the immediate ancestors of the present parishioners whose photographs and memoirs comprise the greater part of this book.

The Villages of Cornwood and Lutton

Cornwood Square, 1876.

*Old Road,
Lutton c. 1910.*

From 1000BC, for nearly 3000 years, the parish has been inhabited, and throughout this time has provided work and a unique way of life for all who lived here. The first known inhabitants settled here in the Bronze Age and the northern moorland part of the parish retains evidence of their way of life in hut circles, field systems, boundary markers and ritual monuments.

The Conqueror's Domesday survey of 1086 noted three manors that we still know today: *Cornehude-Cornhooe* (Cornwood, now Delamore); *Blacheurde* (Blatchford); and *Fernendelle* (Fardel)

Delamore, from Gibb Hill.

Blachford, across the lake.

Fardel, with Headon Down beyond.

THE VILLAGES

In the early Middle Ages the village of Cornwood grew up around the church of St Michael and All Angels. The inhabitants mined the tin on Dartmoor or worked the land of the various manors. Later other manor houses were established: Cholwich Town and Slade.

Natural and human disasters took their toll of even the most rural areas: the Black Death in the 14th century led to abandoned and ruined farmsteads, while the Civil War, when Charles I is said to have hidden in Clergy Cottages, led to conflict and division between villagers.

St Michael and All Angels, from a postcard dated 1910.

Below left: *Slade.*

Below right: *The early moorland house at Cholwichtown.*

Old Clergy House, reputed to be one of the oldest cottages in Cornwood. It was thatched until the 1930s.

Cornwood is the second largest parish in the county of Devon and was even larger at one time before land was given to 'Ivy Bridge' for housing an orphanage (now Dame Hannah Rogers school) and for newly commenced industries, including the paper mill.

The village of Cornwood stands on the junction of an old trade route from Totnes to Tavistock and from the port of Plymouth to the moorland communties that made a living from wool, tin and raising cattle. The Inn at the crossroads by the Square would have been a vital stopping place.

The Cornwood Inn, from a postcard picture taken around the turn of the century. At one time it was known as the Tavistock Inn.

Much of the land in the north of the parish is moorland where the rivers Erme and Yealm rise and where cattle and sheep graze as they have done from earliest times. Since the late nineteenth century china clay has been quarried, an industry which continues until the present day.

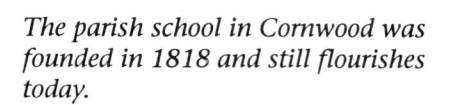

The parish school in Cornwood was founded in 1818 and still flourishes today.

THE VILLAGES

In 1866 Cornwood Station was opened on the Great Western Railway. The deep-cut valleys of the moorland fringe posed problems for the engineers and when the railway came to Cornwood it needed two viaducts.

By the end of the Victorian era shops, a post office, a bakery and club house were established and the population of the parish grew, with cottages built for clay miners and farm workers. Below left: Hillside Cottages, Lutton, previously known as Spion Kop, named after the battle of the Boer War.

Above: *Rowan Cottage, Bond Street.*

Wayside, Fore Street, Cornwood. The far part of the building used to be a shop.

As the present century progressed so the villages of Lutton and Cornwood increased in size, and in 1953 the main street even had electric light installed! As late as 1957 there was still a farm in Bond Street and cattle were driven home along that road.

The present area of Cornwood and Lutton is sixteen square miles and includes over 400 households. Newtown and Crossways in Cornwood, Longfield and Chipple Park in Lutton have provided housing since the First World War and, more recently, Abbotts Park in Cornwood. Fred Willcocks remembers when number one Abbotts Park was the old quarry. Earlier there had been a pound behind 3 and 4 Churchtown, and the field was known as Pound Park, and only later as Quarry Park. Carts would bring stone from the quarry to dump it in 'the square', at the entrance to Abbotts Park, where men would crush it.

The present population of the whole parish, approximately 1000, has not changed greatly over the past half century. It continues to support farming families, and a worldwide china clay industry, whilst contributing to the life of an ever-expanding city to the west, Plymouth, and Ivybridge, a thriving town to the east.

Above left: *Will Kerslake bringing his cow down Bond Street, c. 1957. The cow grazed in a small field past North Cottage on the road to Heathfield. Cross Farm is now known as Rowan Cottage.* Above right: *Yondertown Square, Lutton c. 1910*

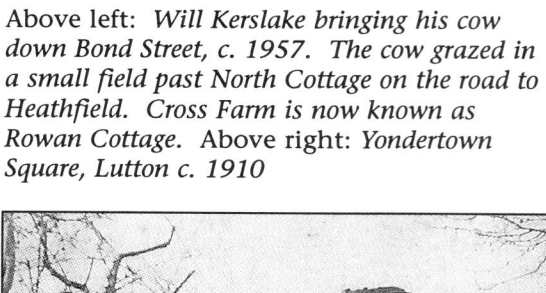

Above: *Higher Torr Cottages as they were before renovation.*

Left: *Almshouse Cottages c. 1890, viewed looking towards Lutton.*

The Cornwood Parish Council

On the 4th December 1894 a Parish Meeting of the Parochial Electors of the Parish of Cornwood was held at the National School, Cornwood for the purpose of electing its first Parish Council. From the minutes of that meeting: "It was proposed, seconded and carried that the Vicar, the Rev. J. T. Mundy be Chairman of the Parish Meeting. Twenty-one Nomination Papers were handed in, numbered and examined, and none were found invalid. The names were placed in alphabetical order and read out. Questions were asked of those standing for election and a show of hands resulted in eleven gentlemen being declared elected". Cornwood had its first Parish Council.

The first meeting of this newly-formed Council was held on the 31st December 1894. William Harvey was elected Chairman and Henry Skelley vice-Chairman. Mr John Colton was appointed Clerk, and Mr Thomas Bulteel, of the Naval Bank, Plymouth, was appointed Treasurer.

One hundred and three years after William Harvey's election, in 1997, Cornwood's first woman Chairman, Mrs Barbara Thomas, assumed office. The first woman to be elected to the Parish Council was Elsie Mary Eggins Wotton of Great Stert, who served from 1949 to 1958.

Mrs Barbara Thomas, 1997 (by permission of Mike Lewis).

So what do these chosen people achieve? More than is often suspected. Over the years they have been concerned with such things as flood water, rights of way. rubbish disposal, and bus shelters. The seat you rest on, and the children's play area, the commemorative tree and preservation of local monuments, could all be there in some part due to the Parish Council.

The Lutton and Cornwood Magazine

If you need a plumber, or hair cut, vet services or dry cleaners, details of clubs, shows or meetings then the place to seek the information is the *Cornwood and Lutton Magazine*. But it hasn't always been so. The earliest known magazine was dated 1870. It was entitled the *Cornwood Magazine*, consisted of one sheet and was included in the *Ivybridge Magazine*. Written by the Vicar it was almost entirely on church affairs. It continued as a single sheet for several years, and in 1895 subscribers could have their copies for the year bound into a single volume.

February 1965, saw a big change. The *Cornwood and Lutton Magazine*, essentially for the villages, was launched, and 200 copies printed, with a circulation of 186, each costing 4d. The first editors were the Rev. William Hamley and Bertram Small. The magazine had an attractive cover, and the communication channel for everyone was born.

In 1978 the Magazine Committee was formed thus spreading the responsibility for a publication that is non-profit making, though donations are received and magazine subscriptions and advertisements provide a source of income to pay for printing, stationery and postage.

The magazine has an important part to play in the life of the people, and long may it continue!

The cover of the magazine from 1965-68.

St Michael's Church before 1898. Beyond the church on the right is the old Pound House.

St Michael's Church 1995.

The Parish Church of St Michael's and All Angels

The church stands on a slight eminence 400 feet above sea level, the highest point in the area of the village except for the site of the original manor house at The Mount. It is about 400m from the crossroads which is now the centre of the village of Cornwood and 1km from the village of Lutton. The building consists of a chancel, the nave and two aisles, each divided from the nave by four pillars of monolithic granite and responds, and there are two transepts (the following quotations in italics are from *Cornwood Notes*).

The general style of the church is Perpendicular, probably the result of restoration at the time of Bishop Grandison, and it is recorded in the Bishop's register that on 19th June, 1336, he dedicated the church, high altar and two others. The site of one of these other altars is shewn by a credence in the east end of the north aisle, while probably the third was in a corresponding position in the south aisle, though no trace of it exists... . A proof that the aisles were not part of the original church, but were added at a later date, may be found in the fact that the East wall of the South aisle conceals half the arch of the Priests' doorway, and it is probable that they formed part of the restoration at that time.

The tower is undoubtedly the oldest part of the Church and its slightly tapering staircase, with remains of lancet windows, shews that it is at least as old as the early English period. In an old map of Dartmoor... the church is represented as having a low spire.

The waggon roof of the nave and aisles is of a type common in the West of England, with panels of plaster between the ribs, and bosses of oak at their juncture, but the Chancel roof which is panelled with oak, is modern.

The only old woodwork is the Jacobean Pulpit. The Rood-screen was destroyed in Puritan times, but the doorways in the North wall mark the entrances to the staircase and Rood-loft.

The Chancel was handsomely restored in 1867 by Lord Blachford, with a Derbyshire alabaster and Italian marble Reredos and arcading, and with Altar-rails of alabaster supported by clustered columns of richly coloured local stone

A later restoration took place in 1875, when choir stalls were fixed, a Lectern given... and the old pews discarded in favour of the present seats, and it was

The Jacobean pulpit.

then agreed by those who claimed ancient rights to some of these pews, that they should be unappropriated henceforth. It was probably at this time that the six carved and gilded 'musical angels' were added on the stone corbels below the principal rafters of the barrel roof of the chancel.

The old pews referred to were probably those mentioned in a document at the end of the seventeenth century when there were seats for different groups of people. The gentry sat facing inwards below the chancel opposite the north and south aisles in box pews and the principal farmers in the middle of the church facing the altar. Behind them, probably on benches, were the single women and widows in the north aisle and the labouring families filled in the back.

The windows all have comparatively modern tracery and glass, as Walter Shute, an intruder into the living in the middle of the 17th century, had permitted the Church to be much abused, the Rood-loft to be pulled down, and the painted windows to be broken in pieces.

The list of 53 incumbents, with notes of the ecclesiastical history of the parish, on the inside south wall by the porch begins with John de Langeford, instituted as Rector before 1263.

The change of title from Rector to Vicar is explained by the fact that in the year 1432 the Rectorial Tithes which had been part of the stipend of the Incumbents were in a high handed way taken from the benefice and devoted to the upkeep of Exeter Cathedral choir, and this arrangement continued till 1742, when they were sold by the Priest Vicars to Sir John Rogers.

The date of the induction of Henry Smith, the 28th incumbent, is not recorded, but it was shortly before the Rebellion. He was much loved by the parish and the neighbouring gentry and is said to have been a man of learning and a zealous loyalist. But loylalty was his undoing as, owing to it, his benefice was sequestrated by the evil powers which had the mastery at the time.

He was subject to much persecution, his goods were plundered, and he and his wife and children had to flee for their lives. Eventuallly he was caught and imprisoned in the neighbourhood of Plymouth, and finally sent to the common gaol at Exeter, where he died, and it is said that his end was hastened by the news of the death of Charles I. It is related that during his incumbency, Cornwood received a royal visitor in the person of Prince Charles who had come to shew his regard to the Vicar, so well-known for his true and faithful adherence to the cause of his beloved master Charles I.

When Henry Smith had been ousted, Walter Shute in defiance of right and justice, was placed in possession of the benefice. It was he of whom Walker in his 'Sufferings of the Clergy' speaks as being a very ignorant and gluttonous fellow, and it is said that on the Martyrdom of Charles I he preached a blasphemous sermon in which he derided Kings and Princes. However he conformed at the Restoration and by the clemency of the Government was allowed to continue in the living, being instituted on the 8th November 1662.

In later times the Church was the scene of shameful disorder, and Waltham Savery, of Slade, was convicted of 'chiding and brawling in the Church and Church yard', and was forbidden to enter it until he should ask pardon of Sir John Rogers publicly and in Church. This he did on St Bartholomew's Day, 1734, with these words: 'Whereas I have been lately convicted by sentence in the Consistory Court of Exon., for chiding and brawling in the Church and Churchyard, I do now acknowledge to have transgressed the Law and offended, for which I ask your pardon'.

The CASE of Sir John Rogers, on an Appeal to a Court of Delegates, to be relieved against a Sentence obtained by Waltham Savery Esq; in the Archdeacon of Totnes's Court, and two Confirmations thereof in the Consistory Court of Exon, and Court of Arches, against Sir John Rogers's Lady, Daughter, and Servants.

SIR JOHN ROGERS, being the Proprietor of an Estate called The Bartons of Wisdom and Blachford, in the County of Devon (formerly the Inheritance of the Family of the Heles, and late of Sir John Rogers deceased, Father of the present Sir John) had, by virtue thereof, a Right to two several Pews in the Church of Cornwood, that belonged to this Estate, and went with it as Part of the Freehold; and to all the antient and accustomed Rights and Privileges which the former Proprietors of this Estate, were entitled to, and enjoyed with the said Pews.

THE Pins and Nails in these Seats, used for hanging of Hats, being in the same Places where they have been for upwards of fifty Years past, and constantly used by the Proprietors of the Seats for the hanging of Hats during the time of Divine Service, without any Complaint, or Pretence of Complaint, from any of the other Sitters, either in the South Isle, or any part of the Church of Cornwood; the present Sir John Rogers and his Family (as they had an undoubted Right to do) usually hung their Hats in the time of Divine Service, in the Church of Cornwood, on these Nails and Pins, which had always, beyond the Memory of Man, been made use of for that purpose.

MR. SAVERY (at whose Promotion the several Presentments in the Archdeacon's Court, herein after mentioned, were made) has also two Seats in this Church, adjoining, or very near Sir John Rogers his Seats, in which Mr. Savery himself and his Family have sat about twenty Years past; during all which Time, and for many Years before, the present Sir John Rogers or his Family, either of the constantly hung their Hats on those Pins and Nails, which had been so long used for that Purpose, without any Complaint from Mr. Savery, or any other Sitters in the Church.

BUT some time in the Year 1723, Mr. Savery on a sudden pretended, that by Sir John's Lady and Daughter (who usually hung the Hats of Sir John's younger Children on the Pins in Sir John's Seat) and by Sir John's Servants hanging of Hats in the manner they did, Mr. Savery, as well as other Sitters in the South Isle of the Church, were deprived of having a Sight or View of the officiating Minister, and of hearing Divine Service: And about Michaelmas 1723, upon a Sunday in the Afternoon, without giving any previous Notice whatsoever to Sir John Rogers or his Family, either of the pretended Offence by their hanging of Hats in that manner, or any Intimation to desist that Practice, as offensive or injurious to Mr. Savery, or any other of the Sitters in the South Isle, in a very violent outrageous manner, and with many Oaths and Imprecations (without any Leave or Order from the Ordinary, or Consent of Sir John, who was then at Plimouth) with a Hook, or Hedging-Bill, cut down all the Pins and Nails in Sir John's and his Servants Pews.

IMMEDIATELY after this, left Sir John should present Mr. Savery for such unwarrantable and injurious Behaviour, instead of making or proposing any Recompence to Sir John, Mr. Savery commenced four litigious vexatious Prosecutions, by preferring four different and separate Presentments in the Archdeacon of Totnes's Court; one against Lady Rogers, another against her Daughter, another against Charles Hawkins one of Sir John's Servants, and another against Charles Harris one other of Sir John's Servants: Whereas one Presentment would have been sufficient to have tried the Right of this Custom and Usage, if Mr. Savery had thought himself really injured by it, and had been his Intention in preferring these Presentments

Dated 14 October 1723, 'The case of Sir John Rogers against Waltham Savery, on Appeal to a Court of Delegates'.

He was the cause of further trouble, for he cut down the pegs on which Sir John and his family hung their hats. Whereupon Dame Mary, her daughter and two servants hung them on a parclose screen. He then brought an action against Sir John which was given in his favour in the Archdeacon's Court in Totnes, but when the case was carried by Sir John on appeal to the Court of Delegates, the previous decision was reversed, and Savery was sentenced to pay £300.

Against the South wall of the Slade Chapel, there is the Cole monument which is an altar tomb without name or inscription. This has in recent years been turned round and now forms the altar in the Chapel. *It is doubtless in memory of Philip Cole of Slade who died on 30th January 1596. He married Joane, the daughter of Thomas Williams of Stowford in the parish of Harford, Speaker in the House of Commons in the reign of Queen Elizabeth. She also desired to be buried in the parish of Cornwood, near the body of her first husband Philip Cole, and her* executors erected a framework of stone above the tomb of Philip enclosing two kneeling figures in the richly coloured dress of the period representing her and Philip.

On the south wall of the Chancel there is a monument consisting of two alabaster figures in Elizabethan costume, a gentleman kneeling on a cushion at a prayer desk facing a lady who is kneeling on the other side. Underneath is inscribed:

Here's rest and peace
Within the grave
Which wee in life
Could never have.

This is surmounted by a shield of arms, quarterly of twenty, and above it the Bellmaine crest, an open hand. In an angle at the NE corner of the Slade Chapel is the monument of John Savery of Slade, an oval tablet of white marble, bearing the following inscription:

Near this place lyeth the body of Mr John Savery,
son of William Savery of Slade, esq.,
by Prudence his wfe, daughter of John Drake of
Iveybridge, esq. ,who departed this life the
21st. Feb. 1695.'

Below this on a black marble tablet is the recumbent figure of a child in a green mantle edged with ermine.

In the entrance to the tower are two tablets which have clearly been moved from their original position in the church recording the deaths of Lady Jane Roll, 1634, and the burial of John Savery (above) buried 27th Feb. 1696 (sic).

Monuments in St Michael's Church. Top left: *The Cole Monument in the Slade Chapel.* Bottom left: *The Bellmaine Monument in the Chancel.* Bottom right: *The Monument to John Savery, 1795.*

The wrought iron gates to the church porch.

The organ dates from 1876 at a cost of c.200 guineas. It is believed to have been built by Father Willis, one of the greatest organ builders of the nineteenth century who built the organs at St Paul's and Exeter Cathedrals amongst others. It is small for the church and may have been moved from its original site in a chapel or private house.

A pair of iron gates for the porch were given as a 'thank offering' by the Short family in 1912. They were made by Francis Walter John Short, a blacksmith with English China Clays at Lee Moor, and were based on the design of the gates at St Mellion Church in Cornwall.

The churchyard is about two acres in extent now and one of the largest in the diocese. A recent survey recorded about 2000 graves, most of them dating from the last 120 years since the original churchyard only extended to about 30 yards below the church. Its present size is due to two gifts of land by the Parker family of Delamore.

The principal entrance to the churchyard is through a handsome lych-gate, given in 1878 by Lord Blachford's sister, Miss Rogers... . In the churchyard there are two altar-tombs belonging to the 17th century. The inscriptions are carved in bold relief. On the tomb near the Lychgate can be read - 'The 5 of Feb., 1639, was buried John Mason of Langum'

(Langham), and on the other - 'The 5th dav of Feb., 1655, Rich the daughter of Mr William Cholwich of Cholwich' - with the family coat of arms on the west end.

West of the tower is the grave of Richard Veal on which is inscribed:

> *Who'er you are who passeth by*
> *As you are, so once was I.*
> *As I am now so you must be,*
> *Prepare for death and follow me.*

The site of the earliest vicarage is not known though there is a reference in a lease of 1655 to 'the Church house of the parish of Cornwood or the house belonging to the parishioners to be erected.... by John Hele (of Wisdome)'. The oldest existing houses associated with the church name are Old Clergy Cottages in Fore Street. These appear to be older than the present Church House at the north side of the churchyard which became a Dame School in the last century and may have replaced the seventeenth century house.

In 1780 the vicar at the time, Rev. Duke Yonge, built a Georgian front on to an existing farmhouse and created the handsome Glebe House, about a mile from the church and looking down the valley of the River Yealm. This remained the vicarage until a new one was built in 1912 not far from the church on the road to Corntown, during the incumbency of Rev. Powning. When the Rev. John Perry left the parish in 1992 the vicarage was sold and a bungalow bought for the future priest-in-charge opposite the church.

There is a single sheet recording baptisms on 4th April 1669, but the oldest continuous register of Baptisms, Marriages and Deaths is in a half-bound volume beginning with the year 1685 and ending in 1783. Some entries are impossible to decipher as the edges of the paper are completely worn out, and others are difficult to read owing to the use of ink which has faded.

Francis Walter John Short who made the church porch gates.

Above: *The churchyard of Cornwood Parish Church, 1875. Robert Lang is sitting next to the grave of Lord Blachford which, with other Blachford graves, was at that time surrounded by wrought iron railings. These no longer exist.*

Left: *The oldest chest tomb is the grave of John Mason of Langum (Langham), 1639. He must have been an important yeoman farmer, and his tomb is in the most conspicuous place immediately above the lych gate. The Inscription reads: 'THE 5 OF FEBRUARY 1639 WAS BURYD JOHN MASON OF LANGHAM.'*

Below: *Glebe House.*

The Choir

The choir must have been started when the choir stalls were fitted in 1875, although it is likely that a choir and orchestra existed before that date. The photo of the choir outing to Bovisand that year records a very special occasion. Since then the numbers in the choir have ebbed and flowed, as in most parishes. At present there are a dozen adults and three girls in the choir who sing at matins once a month and on all the principal festivals of the Church.

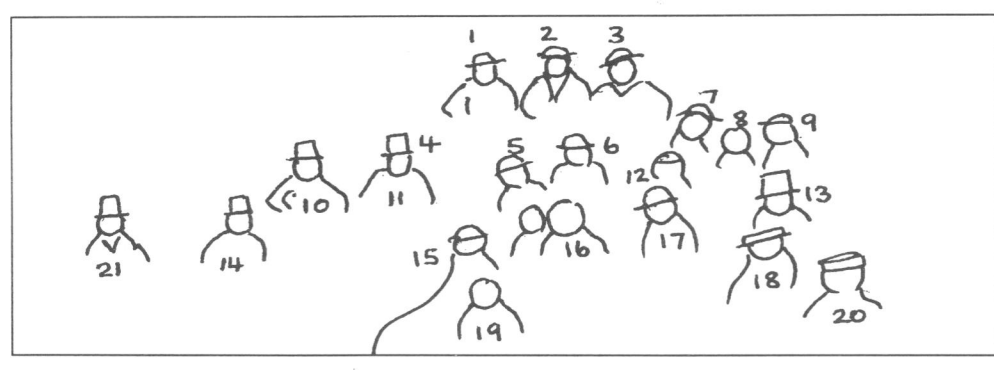

The first choir outing to Bovisand in 1875. Those in the photograph are:
1. J. Vivian
2. Septimus Green
3. M. Mudge
4. R. Mudge
5. S. Mudge
6. A. Bastard
7. F. Vivian
8. A. Parker
9. W. Vivian
10. H. Vivian
11. G. Parker
12. W. Bowden
13. J. Bastard
14. W. Mudge
15. Mrs Bartholemew
16. Rev. Bartholemew
17. A. Vivian
18. Ernest Pode
19. F. B. Brooks
20. C. Budge
21. G. Sanders

St Michael and All Angels choir, 1944.
1. Trow Sercombe; 2. Gordon Nelder; 3. Bob Ham; 4. Bennett Blight; 5. Peter Nelder; 6. Tom Squires; 7. Adrian Phillips; 8. Richard Drew; 9. Peter Mudge; 10. Harold Pryce; 11. Harry Hext; 12. ?; 13. Sidney Atwill; 14. ?; 15. ?; 16. ?; 17. ?; 18. ?; 19. Rev. Coleridge; 20. Bishop of Plymouth; 21. Frank Greep.

The Church Bells

The Tower contains a set of six bells, five of which were cast by Pennngton in 1770 and bear the name of Nicholas Shepherd, churchwarden. The treble bell was added in 1835 and is named after the then incumbent, Reverend W. Oxenham. In the tower is a clock with three faces which Lady Blachford gave in memory of her husband [Cornwood Notes].

The bells, silenced in 1894 due to the deterioration of the bell mechanism, were re-hung and ceremoniously re-opened on 3rd June 1895. The bells were rung regularly, and usually twice on Sunday, until 1939, when an inspection showed that they were too dangerous to ring. The bells were taken down and sent to the foundry of Messrs Taylors of Loughborough where they were tuned and new hangings made. The bells were returned to the tower and rededicated by the Bishop of Exeter at a special service on 13th April 1940. Like all bells in the country they were silenced in 1940 by order and rung again in 1943 when the threat of invasion had passed.

The first ladies joined the Tower in 1969. In 1969 Reg Champ, for many years gardener at Delamore, retired after 50 years ringing at St Michael's.

In 1972 it was decided to hold an invitation ringing competition and since then this has been an annual event bringing 15-17 teams to Cornwood to compete for trophies given in memory of R. Champ, J. Thompson and W. Jonas.

In 1971 ten handbells were donated to the church by Mr & Mrs A. Wotton of Great Stert. A group was formed by Rev. John & Mrs. Ruth Perry, which has since played at Christmas and on other occasions to raise money for various charities. There are now 31 bells so that four-part harmony can be rung. The ringers have taken part in music festivals and have been recorded on 'Plymouth Sound' Radio.

The Cornwood ringers win the shield at the ringing festival of 1945. Left-right: *Jim Shepherd; Burt Jeffery; Reg Champ; Arch Reglar; Jack Thompson; Jim Stacey.*

Henry Bidgood

On the outer wall of the south side of the chancel of St Michael's is a stone recording the death of Henry Bidgood on '27 Jany 1738', with a skull and crossbones. Many children have thought this meant that he was a pirate or perhaps a highwayman.

This type of memorial stone occurs in some other parishes and the reason for it is not known for certain. Some think it is a sign that he died childless, others that it is merely a reminder that death comes to all of us. It is also suggested that the person may have died of the plague in which case he would have to be buried beyond the parish boundary but might be specially remembered by his parish church.

The most likely explanation is one given by Rev. Hamley, a former vicar. In olden days the village carpenter, the principal craftsman, made coffins and was often the undertaker. He was also sometimes the monumental mason whose sign or trade mark was the skull and crossbones. If so, he is likely to have made some of the memorials in the church such as the one to the first Sir John Rogers and his wife.

Charities

The Yonge Charity

Rev. Duke Yonge, a former vicar, founded the Yonge Charity (in 1811). He left certain lands at Lutton and a sum of money to trustees for the benefit of the poor of the parish, and directed that one part of this endowment should be devoted, among other things, to the education of a certain number of poor children of the parish, to be selected by the Vicar, and to the teaching of the Catechism and principles of the Church of England, and another part to the purchase of Bibles, Testaments and Religious Tracts published by the SPCK to be distributed in the parish.

The Dame school, now known as Church House, on the north side of St Michael's church, formed part of the endowment of the Charity. In 1875 a small School-room for infants was built by some of the Landowners of the parish at Lutton on land belonging to the Yonge Charity Trust and subsequently an addition was made by Admiral Parker to form a Chancel and Vestry for use when the room was required for Divine Service. In 1885 Lord Blachford built a house for the School-teacher on land belonging to the same trust. [Cornwood Notes].

The trustees consist of two ex-officio trustees - the Vicar of Cornwood and the owner of the Puslinch estate (the Yonge family) - four trustees nominated by the Parish Council, and three co-optative trustees appointed by resolution.

The Rooke Charity

Known properly as the Cornwood Parish Lands Charityals, it is also referred to as the Wakeham's Rooke Charity and the Cornwood Relief-in-need Charity. It was founded in 1700 by the Fortescues of Hangar, who conveyed to trustees a messuage and tenement called East Rooke, alias Reed's or Wakeham's Rooke, and the rent of this farm is now spent at Christmas on blankets, coal and clothing.

In 1969 Wakehams Rooke Farm was sold. The capital was invested and in 1972 the Trust Deed of the charity was changed with the approval of the Charity Commissioners to avoid giving unwanted gifts in the form of coal, and so that help could be given with the cost of other forms of heating and alternative necessities. The trustees can help with the purchase of tools, of books and fees for educational purposes and for travelling expenses to help people to earn a living.

The trustees consist of the Vicar, ex-officio, two nominated by the Parish Council and up to five co-opted by resolution of the trustees.

The Underwood Memorial Congregational Church, Lutton

The Congregational Church, including the Sunday School, was founded in Lutton on Palm Sunday in 1853, by Mr Richard Peek of Hazelwood, near Kingsbridge, as the records say 'to bring the Gospel into the dark and benighted village of Lutton'.

In 1903, it was found that the building then in use, now known as the Sunday School, was quite inadequate. This situation was made known to the Plymouth Congregational Council, then the Three Towns Congregational Council.

Mr E. R. Lester, the Treasurer of the Council, purchased and gave the land on which, later, the church was erected, the cost of the land being £50. A building fund was started, and every member subscribed raising a total of £100. Then, by bazaars and fund raising events, the total was increased to £200 and in 1909 the Building Fund was formed with Mr G. H. Widger as Chairman and Mr T. R. Whittley as Secretary. March 15th 1911 saw the Foundation Stone laid by Mr E. R. Lester, and the church was built by Ambrose Andrews of Plymouth at the cost of £1150.00.

The great day of Opening and Dedication, to the Glory of God, came on September 13th 1911 at 3.15pm. The Church was opened by Mrs Thomas Richard Whittley.

Many sums, large and small, had been added to defray the cost, but the church was to open with a debt of £400. To the great joy of everyone, on the opening day it was announced that Mr John T Underwood of New York, a son of the founder member, John Underwood, who was on his way by sea from America, had communicated to say that he would be pleased to make a gift of £400, and the church was opened free of debt: truly a Free Church! It was then decided, in appreciation, to call the church 'The Underwood Memorial Congregational Church'. Mr John Underwood visited the church shortly afterwards and took part in a morning service.

The occasion of the opening was one of great rejoicing. The whole neighbourhood turned out in their Sunday best clothes, and over 500 had tea in a marquee. The Sunday School scholars formed a guard of honour and the procession was led by

The Underwood Memorial Congregational Church, Lutton, opened 1911. Affectionately called Lutton Chapel.

the Cornwood Brass Band. The dedication and sermon was given by the Rev. Justin Evans of Southernhay Congregational Church, Exeter, and the evening meeting was presided over by Mr Gerard N. Ford, Chairman of the Congregational Union Of England and Wales. The organist and choirmaster was Mr William Rendle who held this office for over fifty years. He was self-taught, and the church organ was a harmonium.

Mr Bertram F Small has served at the church as Lay Preacher, Sunday School Teacher, and Lay Pastor for over 50 years and still is today.

Within the church is a War Memorial which is the same as that in the parish church, Cornwood. This is a very unusual feature in a free church.

The top photograph shows the interior of Lutton Chapel before the First World War. The war memorial now occupies the alcove on the right hand side. The lower photograph, taken in 1997, shows the organ and pulpit which were moved into their present position in the late 1930s. Electric lighting was installed in January 1942.

Thomas Henry Skidmore was Church Treasurer from 1908 to 1944. with a break of three years, while in Canada. He was also a Lay Preacher and Sunday School Superintendent. Mr Skidmore worked as a fore-man and china clay worker at Stockers Works on Headon Down and was involved in many local activ-ities. During the 1939-45 war he became the billeting officer for Lutton, and was known to the evacuees as Uncle Tom. He was very generous with his time and his money. helping all in need. The Cornwood Parish Council, and the Plympton St Mary Rural District Council, gained benefit from his work with them and he was an active committee member of the Lutton Co-operative Society.

Golden Jubilee (1911-1961) of the Underwood Memorial Congregational Church, Lutton. The service was held on 13 September 1961. From left: 1. Rev.W. P. Weight (Vicar of Cornwood). 2. Mr William Francis Small (Church Secretary). 3. Mr W. 0. Pippin. 4. Rev. Charles A. Haig. 5. Rev. Frank E. Quick. 6. Mr Bertram Small (Lay Pastor of Lutton Chapel).

Lutton Sunday School Centenary - 1853 to 1953. From left - back row: 1. Bert Small 2. Bryan Rendle 3. Tony Stancombe 4. Frank Small 5. Mr Clifford Small 6. Mrs Ethel Warley 7. Mr Edgar Rendle 8. Terry Beaver. Next to back row: 1. Mrs Barbara Small 2. Deanna McNeil 3. Wendy Bloomfield 4. Rosemary Happle 5. Janet McNeil 6. Monica Small 7. Shirley Warley. Next to front row: 1. Alan Warley 2. Deirdre McNeil 3. Gloria Skelley 4. Ann Blackshaw 5. Christine Furber 6. Dennis Warley 7. Robert McNeil. Front row: 1. Alan Mudge 2. David Bloomfield 3. Sandra Keast 4. Marilyn Skidmore 5. Jimmy Mudge 6. Jimmy Underwood 7. Susan Mudge 8. Ian Devine 9. Rosalind Skelley. Very front: 1. David Furber 2. Graham Baskerville.

A memorial stone, in memory of John Underwood, laid when Lutton Congregational Church was built.

Lutton Sunday School, Old Road, Lutton. Founded 1853.

Farms and Farming

One of the attractions of living in Cornwood is that most of the inhabitants are able to see green fields out of at least one window of their house, even in 1997. Farmers, their families and farmhands have worked the three thousand or so acres of agricultural land and grazed their stock on the surrounding moorland for generations.

The influence of farming on the appearance of the countryside is immense and layers of history are reflected in the rural landscape. According to the Doomsday survey of 1086 much of the parish to the north was then 'waste' of scrub and woodland, which was later colonised by free peasants in the twelfth and thirteenth centuries.

The original boundaries of their farms are still marked by the lanes which fan out in the upper valley of the Yealm river, bounded to the North by High House Moor, Dendles Wood and Watercombe Waste.

The ruined farm at High House is, as the name implies, the one farthest out upon the moor. It was probably abandoned after the Black Death which impoverished the countryside in 1349, but it still gives an idea of the layout and size of an early farmstead.

Most of the land was owned by the three large estates: Cornwood (now called Delamore), Blachford and Slade. These very large acreages were gradually divided into separate holdings with a farmhouse and out-buildings. The earliest of the farmhouses is Cholwich Town which dates from around 1500. This farm was held by the Cholwich family from soon after 1200 until 1835. Several other farmhouses date from the seventeenth century, or much earlier: Hanger and Little Stert, which are now private dwellings, and Wisdome, Lower Hele and Moor which are still working farms.

Cholwichtown Farm.

Wisdome Farm

The main dwelling and the stables opposite are said to have been built in 1564 and the granite mullioned windows there tend to confirm this. But the original farmhouse by the road has three doorways with pointed arches of granite which suggest a much earlier date for this building with its kitchen, cellar, granary and loft. The farm was bought by John Rogers in 1690, four years before he bought Blachford. He paid £2,700 for Wisdome.

Cost of building Wisdome (all materials and labour charges itemised on costing in the Devon Record Office)

1627	£437.16.4
1628	£369.5.2
1629	£139.7.9
1630	£219.12.2
1631	£94.00.9
1632	£119.5.1
1633	£133.19.2
1634	£94.1.3
1635	£76.17.0
1636	£71.2.6
1637	£107.16.11
1638	£104.8.4
1639	£79.19.9
1640	£80.19.9
1640	£80.19.I
1641	£60.7.5
1642	£5718.9

Total :15 years at a cost of £2246.17.5

Lutton Farm

Wisdome has been farmed by the Andrew family since before the Second World War.

Sherrell Farm

The farmyard at Sherrell.

Moor Farm

Moor Farm has been occupied by the Northmore family since 1940. The farmhouse has an interesting granite fireplace, the lintel decoratively carved with the inscription 'ANODO 1657' and with a shield bearing the initials MWM.. Who was the MWM who lived at the farm all those years ago? Was he possibly related to the Masons of Langham? The stone is said to come from a now disused quarry, near Pithill on Hanger Down, which produced a high quality pink granite.

Wilkey's Moor Farm

Wilkey's Moor is no longer a working farm but is a fine example of an isolated settlement in the moorland landcsape.

Higher Hele Farm

The house is probably of the 16th century, but was re-fashioned, and the front rebuilt in the 18th century. The result is a most beautifully proportioned facade. There is a slate hipped roof over the five windows which are placed symmetrically across the first floor level, and divided from the ground floor by a flat string course of granite stonework.

The ground floor windows are centred with those on the first floor, with a central porch over the main entrance with its own slated roof and approached up three stone steps.

The doorway at the back of Higher Hele reveals that this is a much earlier part of the building. The proportions of the doorway and the windows here, and the carved granite, speak highly of the 16th century craftsmen who built it

FARMS AND FARMING

THE FARMING SCENE

In 1850 forty people were listed as farmers, ten of them called Horton, but they were not all related to each other. There is a descendant of the Uppaton and Houndle branch of the family still farming in the village, and that is Alan Pearse of Delamore Farm.

Eleven larger farms were also listed, of those Cholwichtown, Fardel, Lutton, Uppaton and Wisdome are still working farms. Most of the larger farms employed a man. Only Blachford, where the home farm was kept in hand, could afford a larger workforce.

Harvest time at Blachford, the late 1940s. Left-right: *Norman Willcocks, Bert Shepherd, Tony Mills, George Willcocks (commonly known as 'Lightning'), Michael Borokof, and Tom Balkwill.*

Wages for a worker during the 1920s was a pound a week, with half a day off each week.

In the early part of the twentieth century Blachford, Slade and Delamore Estates let their farms. This was a very good system as it enabled many who were not from a farming family to become established on the farming ladder. Nowadays, many of the Blachford and Slade farms have been sold to the sitting tenants and the Delamore farms have been amalgamated as tenants have retired.

During the first half of this century, and long before, all of the farmers would have carried out a mixed farming enterprise. They would have had a few milking cows, a couple of breeding sows, and poultry to keep the farmer's wife busy. Beef, sheep and ponies would be the natural product of

FARM WAGES

5s. a Week Increase Recommended

The Central Agricultural Wages Board has recommended an increase in the minimum wage from 65s. to 70s. per week.

This recommendation will now go before the county committees.

Notification of a rise in agricultural workers' wages. From the South Devon Times, *December 1944.*

this moorland village. Most would also have grown some corn and root crops to feed their animals in winter.

There are some 6000 acres of woodland and moorland in the parish and most of the farms enjoyed grazing rights. Farmers of the Delamore estate were allotted areas on Penn Moor and the Blachford tenants used Stall Moor. These areas were designated by the landlord and a 'Moor Man' was appointed by him to ensure that no one encroached upon another Commoner's rights. Frederick Sowden of West Rooke Farm was the last Moor Man for Delamore, and Mr Luscombe of Hall Farm was the last to act for Blachford. Their function died out after the Second World War.

Reg Steer can recall Stall Moor being rented from Blachford in the 1920s by John Munford, who allowed cottagers to graze their ponies for one shilling per year. To identify a pony the owner punched a hole in the animal's ear and threaded a coloured ribbon through it. On Sunday mornings Jack Willcocks of Lee Moor would ride his pony around Stall Moor to check that all the ponies were still there.

Until the mid-thirties the moor was grazed by the indigenous breed of Dartmoor sheep, then Scotch sheep were gradually introduced. The cattle, both on the moor and home on the farm, were big brown South Devons along with a few highland cattle. Now there are a wide variety of breeds grazing the moor, both British and European. Once a year there came the cattle drift, followed by a pony drift the week after, when all animals were cleared from the moor.

The moor also provided ferns (bracken) which was cut and dried and stored in ricks to be used for bedding animals during the winter.

Charlie Willcocks at West Rooke, with newborn quad lambs.

David Skelley takes a pig down the road to Berry's Farm with his dog, Meg.

Sid Phillips at Stone in the 1950s.

Reg German

Ploughing at Rooke in the 1950s. Reg Steer is driving the near tractor with John Munford behind. The wood in the background no longer exists.

FARMING TOOLS AND METHODS

The shire or heavy horse was the farmer's faithful servant for hundreds of years and many in the parish can still recall working with them. Basil Sharp remembers ploughing with Laddie and Violet at West Rooke when he was a farmer's boy in the 1950s. Two horses pulling a single furrow plough would plough an acre a day. Some farmers hereabouts tried to speed things up by using two furrows and three horses and managed up to 2 acres per day. However, it was still a slow and laborious task by today's standards when a modern tractor and four furrow plough can manage at least eight acres a day.

Horses were used for every task on the farm and were very busy at harvest time. The pictures on the following pages show how hay was made. It was swept into the stack with a sweep, and then winched on to the rick using a haypole and grab. Thatched ricks of loose hay were a familiar sight in pre-war days until balers were invented.

Corn harvest was another big event in the farming calendar. It was cut and bound into sheaves by a binder. The sheaves were then put into stooks and left to dry. In theory it took about eight days to be dry enough to cart but it could be made difficult with our English summers and being on high ground near Dartmoor. The sheaves were made into ricks and stored until it was needed. During the course of the winter the grain was threshed from the straw to be used for food and bedding for the cattle.

Howard German watching blacksmith Mr Hallet and his son making ready to shoe 'Joe' at Wakeham's Rooke.

Reg German and Gordon Rendle.

Workers in the hayfields, 1931. From left, standing: *Jim Steer (woodsman); Sid Stephens (carpenter);* Middle row: *Frank Hurd (gamekeeper); Fred Turpin.* Front row: *Fred Turpin's brother, George Crimp (groom).*

The 1940s: One of four haystacks that used to be made each year at Bridge Farm

Haymaking

Reg German and Gordon Rendle stacking hay on to a rick from the hay wagon.

Left and below: *Two photographs showing a double horse hay sweep. This was dragged around the field scooping up the hay that had been previously cut and left to dry. In the background to each picture can be seen the part-made rick with the hay pole around which the rick was constructed, using a simple grab to lift the hay up to the top of the rick. In the lower photograph, William Wotton is sitting behind the sweep. Working in the background are Andrew Wotton, Bill Downing and the Williams boys from Venton.*

Harvesting

Farmers had to help each other at harvest time as it was a very labour-intensive job and this usually turned into a social occasion. Either tea was taken into the field and everyone sat around, or they all ended up in the farmhouse kitchen around a long table laden with home-cooked food. The catering on one farm however, was a little different. Soup was brought out to the men in a bucket and placed on the ground, everyone then dipped their mugs in and helped themselves. No soup ladles here! The dogs had their share and then the men came along for seconds. Ugh!

BEST HARVEST IN LIVING MEMORY IN SOUTH DEVON
September 2nd 1955

This year's harvest has been the best in living memory, claim many South Devon farmers. Exceptionally fine weather at the right time, the absence of rabbits and other advantages have made the yield an unexpectedly heavy one.

'All we want now is a good fall of rain,' they say. Mr J H Stephens, of Higher Hele Farm, Cornwood, expressed the view of many others when he told the South Devon Times, *'This has been a simply wonderful year; we have had a marvellous time with all our crops. First we had the sun to ripen the wheat, barley oats and other crops, just when we wanted it, and since then we have had ideal weather to enable us to bring it in. This year I found I could not do a thing wrong! There is no doubt about it', he continued, 'I cannot remember a better harvest.'*

Rust, the disease that has caused anxiety in other areas, had not affected Mr Stephen's wheat to any noticeable extent.

The effect of the complete lack of rabbits had come to him as a great surprise.

'I never would have imagined that rabbits did so much damage,' he remarked. 'This year I have got six bags of corn from the first cut around the edge of a field that was previously affected by rabbits. On an average year the yield on the first round would be only two bags. Even the average man-in-the-street could see the difference that the absence of rabbits has made.'

Caterpillars, however, were a nuisance. Kale, turnips, cabbages and root crops in general had all suffered. 'They are a real plague,' Mr Stephens complained.

Harvesting at Blachford 1931. Elsie Crimp, wife of George Crimp, groom at Blachford is sitting on a pook of hay. Daughter, Elsie stands at the field's edge.

A horse-drawn binder at work in the fields above Stone c. 1930.

Harvesters pose beside the hay wagon From left: Tom Balkwill of Stone; Bill 'Bimbo' Kerslake of Bond Street; Fred Kerslake of Churchtown.

*Harvesting at Higher Hele in the 1980s.
From left: David Jones, Reg German, Gwen Willcocks, Lee Willcocks, Charles Munford. Back row: Dave Matthews, Albert Willcocks, with Michael Northmore driving the tractor*

Hay harvest at Moor Cross, 1949. From left, back row: *Mrs Greep, Mr Smith (against tree), Victor German (with the horse, Bob).* Middle: *Mr Hosgood, Connie Smith, William Greep, Eleanor Greep, Hilda Greep, Robert Cox, Reg German, Anne German, Michael Stancombe. The boy in front is Peter Smith.*

Harvesting at Bridge Farm, mid 1920s. From left, back row: Ern Bowden, Tom Smerdon, Harry Kingwell. Front row: Mr Luscombe, Minnie Luscombe, Blanche Luscombe, (? carpenter from Cornwood).

Cattle Sales

Cornwood had it's own cattle fair twice a year, in May and September, although this must have been more than a hundred years ago. During the early part of this century cattle and sheep were taken to local markets. There were four, all held in turn on each Monday of the month. New calved cows and calves went to Ivybridge. The calf was put in the trap and the cow followed on behind. Herbert Sharp could remember doing this quite regularly, and also how he used to walk a sow pig from Wisdome to Uppaton, via Blachford, to visit the boar and home again with a satisfied look on it's face.

Other markets were held at Yealmpton, Modbury and the biggest at Plympton, which is the only one to survive although in quite a small way now. Cattle and sheep are sold directly to an abattoir or taken to Exeter market.

Received .... the sum of £30 (thirty pounds)
for two milking cows.

Cyril W. Passy
18 Apr 55

Top: *Cattle sale at Blachford, July 1997.*

Above: *A receipted bill of sale from 1995. Two milking cows for £30!*

Left: *Reg German taking a cow to market, 1957.*

Milk, butter, meat and cider

Milk was sold locally direct from the farm to the villagers. Jimmy Stevens of Higher Hele sold the round to Johnny Glover of Delamore Farm then it passed to Charlie Willcocks at West Rooke. Surplus milk from other farms was either turned into butter and cream or taken to Cornwood Station and put on a train to go to a dairy in Plymouth. Janet Northmore of Moor Farm still makes butter today but now she uses a Kenwood mixer!

Animals were slaughtered at home on the farm for the family to eat. Pork was stored in salt in wooden bins and kept in the cold slate floored room that all farmhouses seemed to have. The present kitchen at Delamore Farm was the slaughter house for the old Delamore House prior to 1850. In the early part of this century Butcher Hillson lived at Wisdome Mill. He used to slaughter sheep, pigs and calves from local farms and take them to Plymouth Market on Thursdays. He would leave home at 4am with his son and the cart loaded with meat and two horses to pull it up Gorah Hill. Once they reached the top the forehorse was unhitched and the son returned with it to Wisdome while Mr Hillson continued the journey to Plymouth.

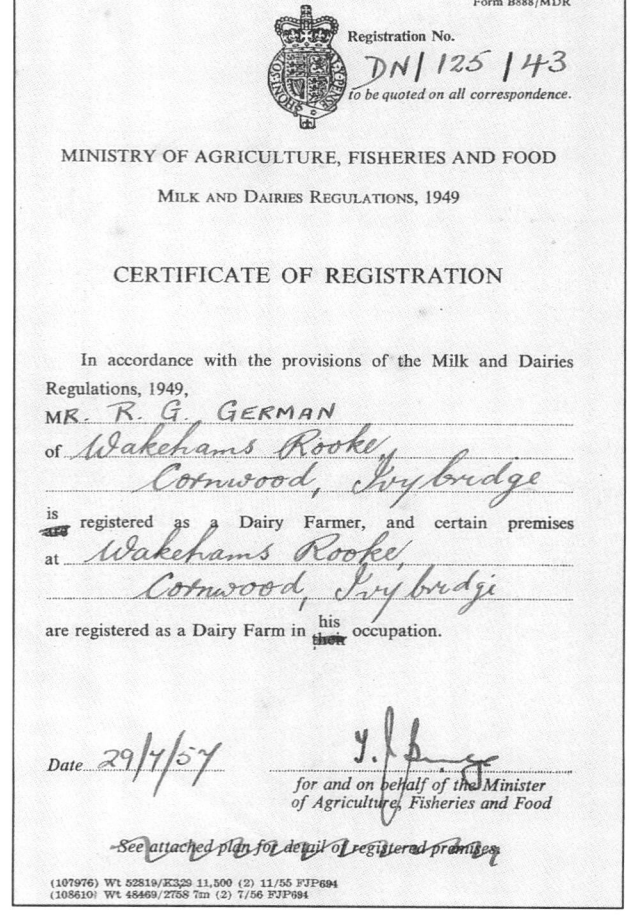

Top left: *Howard German with Guernseys at Wakehams Rooke, 1957.*

Above: *A certificate of registration issued by MAFF to Reg German in 1957.*

Left: *Reg German with Anne, Howard and Barbara Goodall coming through the meadow having taken milk to Blachford, mid 1950s.*

Above: *Friesian dairy herd returning to Fardel from milking, 1950s.*
Right: *Jeremy Dennis of Fardel with a prizewinning high-yield Holstein Friesian, 1996.*

Two things which have a great influence on farmers' lives are tractors and the weather. The tractor first began to appear in this village during the war, when they were fitted with spade lugs instead of tyres. They revolutionised the speed at which farm jobs could be completed, although in the early days some farmers still insisted on the horse doing certain jobs. Nowadays, farmers either have a big new tractor and are kept poor paying for it, or have an old one and spend a lot of time repairing it.

Waterwheels were another source of power on farms the early part of the century. They were used to grind corn, sharpen tools and saw firewood. Most farms had orchards of cider apples and made their own cider with a press such as the one still in existence at Wisdome Farm. Many a good tale has been told over a mug of cider!

Top left: *The Cider press Wisdome Farm. In 1752 Thomas Jarvis and Stephen Bowden agreed to build a new screwpound with runner and layer for cider making and to maintain this for three years at a cost of £3.*
Above: *The waterwheel at Fardel.*
Left: *A cow suckling a pig at Stone, c. 1950. Note the granite trough and the half-tyre version beside it.*

The hunt at Blachford April 1909.

The hunt on Cornwood Common, 1912. Squire Coryton, centre, Master, and Colonel Parker forward right.

The Dartmoor Hunt

The very early history of hunting is difficult to ascertain. What is certain is the pre-eminence of our parish in the history of The Dartmoor Foxhounds. Perhaps the first known writings that mention hunting, is of Thomas Pearse of Fardel and Waltham Savery of Slade. In 1740 both are recorded as keeping a pack of hounds. Indeed it was Mr Savery's huntsman who, dressed in his night attire, was unrecognised by his pack at night, and attacked and devoured by them. The hounds were kept at Slade (hence Kennel Bridge), and it is said that even to this day on a dark night in November... !

Waltham Savery died in 1778 having dissipated a fortune! One of Sir George Treby's sons (who owned Delamore) mentions that his father gave the hounds to John Bulteel of Flete who died in 1801. The huntsman was John Roberts, who was also huntsman in 1806 when John Spurrel Pode of Slade had possession of them. In 1827 John Crocker Bulteel of Lyneham purchased all Mr Pode's hounds and the modern era began with the naming of the Dartmoor Hunt. On his death Mr Bulteel's widow, Elizabeth, gave the pack to his close friend Charles Trelawney of Coldrennick, Liskeard, and the kennels were moved to Ivybridge. The pack was hunted by Thomas Limbatty or Limpity 'the Gypsy Huntsman' who, starting as a terrier boy, hunted without intermission from 1827-1860. He was a determined and utterly fearless horseman whose doings and sayings were the talk of the countryside!

Mr Trelawney hunted hounds for 30 seasons and they were then purchased by Admiral Parker at Delamore in 1887. Despite being a real heavyweight the Admiral had no trouble crossing the moor albeit with a team of helpers! Boxall and Yeo were the huntsmen. On his retirement Admiral Parker was succeeded, in 1899, by his son-in-law William Coryton of Pentillie Castle, St Mellion, and he hunted with the same huntsman, Joe Higman, for over 50 years, with the help and involvement of the first Lord Mildemay of Flete.

During the Great War a committee ran the hunt, with Colonel Parker as Chairman. After the war, the mastership passed to Commander Davey who, having fought in the Great War, hunted for 21 years and was then killed in the Second World

Master Michael Weir and Jonathan Northmore with the Dartmoor Hunt.

War in 1940. Since then there have been 15 masters or joint masters including the well known journalist and comedian R.W.F. 'Willy' Poole in 1964. Also of note was Major Michael Howard who was twice master, and was the grandson of Squire Coryton and great-grandson of Admiral Parker. The present master, Michael Weir, took over from Dr David Mills in 1994 and the kennels have moved to Bittaford.

The hunt still meets twice a week and still has plenty of Cornwood connections. The boundaries have changed little since Mr Trelawney's days but the hunt no longer meets in the centre of Plympton! The hunt still covers over 100 square miles of moorland, and the going varies from impassable bogs to spongy old turf requiring active, well-bred horses and very courageous, able riders. The moor rises to 1800 ft and produces breathtaking views. The weather is still a major problem!

Those who hunt must be tough, resilient and enthusiastic to cope with uncomfortable and frightening times in fog and drizzle - but the rewards are unique.

Left: *Mary Parker on 'Ro-anna' at Blachford, March 1914. An item in* The Times *of 1914 noted:* 'The danger of riding astride from a medical correspondent: Women, as the mother of the race, must on no account jeopardize her ability to perform the function of motherhood, safely and efficiently.'

Below top: *A meet at Moor Cross April 1904. Master, W. Coryton of Pentillie, Cornwall, son-in-law of Admiral Parker.*

Below: *Delamore Meet, March 1969. From left: Gavin Dollard; David Mills (Master); Mrs D.M. Parker, Paul Fermor.*

The hunt gathering outside the Cornwood Inn in the 1950s. The man with folded arms is Tom Kerslake and his wife Peggy stands next to the car and their daughter-in-law Pamela Palmer is in the striped skirt. The lady in the dark dress is Jessie Matthews.

The last hunt to assemble in Cornwood Square, February 1975. The girl at the far left, facing, on horseback is Lucy Cannon (now Chilcott); the lady with the spotted headscarf is Mrs Southby-Taylor; the man to the left of the cross, with arms folded, is Mr Brendan of Waterleat; the girl to the right of the telegaph pole, in front of the Landrover is Chris Passy; in front of her the man in the cap is Reg Steer; the lady behind the near car, wearing a black hat, is Auriol Butler.

Number 1 and 2 Corntown. Built in 1901 by Louisa and Margaret Deare, on land settled on them in 1895 by their relative Annie Matilda Passy, of Blachford. When this photograph was taken, c.1905, the houses were owned by the railway company to house their staff. The traction engine is taking china clay down to Cornwood station. Ida Wingate, aged about 3 years, is standing in the doorway of the house, while her mother and brother Reg watch at the gate, with Mrs Skidmore and baby.

China Clay workers, date unknown, possibly in the 1920s. Frank Bowden is fourth from left.

China Clay
From Cookworthy to Cornwood

Since before the middle of the last century china clay has had a strong influence on the lives of the people of Cornwood and Lutton. It all began when, in 1755, William Cookworthy, the Plymouth chemist, discovered and experimented with china clay. This was an essential raw material for the production of high quality porcelain. By 1795 china clay was being produced in commercial quantities in Cornwall, but it was not until 1827 that a good bed of clay was discovered just west of Lee Moor.

With the opening up of this industry labour was needed, and although experienced clay workers were brought from Cornwall, local manpower also was required. The skills to work the clay were passed through generations of families in local villages such as Cornwood and Lutton, and this tradition continues today.

The industry grew, and vast areas of land were opened up, making the production of china clay a very important part of the economy of the South West. China clay was to be found nowhere else in the British Isles.

Members of the Watts, the Blake and the Bearne families had been involved in the ball clay industry around Newton Abbot since the latter part of the 18th century and by 1861 the company of Watts, Blake and Bearne had been formed and was shipping ball clay to many continental ports from Russia to Spain. By the early 1870s the company moved into the production of china clay and discovered a good bed of this clay at Headon.

This was at the time when a period of depression was beginning to hit the industry and most pits had to reduce production, but the high quality of the product extracted from the Devon pits meant they were able to continue production. As the markets slowly recovered, so employment prospects improved and Cornwood and Lutton families benefited.

With the outbreak of war in 1914, all pits suffered as men left to join the colours, many never to return. In the post-war years some stability returned to the industry continuing through the 1920s, only to be hit by the next depression and once again production dropped. All companies went through hard times, and only those producing clay of the highest quality, survived.

In the early days the majority of the clay produced was used by the ceramics industry but, after the depression, other uses were being discovered, the greatest being for paper filling and paper coating. Sand in vast quantities was a by-product of clay production and by selective grading was finding a market in its own right.

The year 1939 brought the threat of another war and soon, through conscription, many pits lost most of their labour force. In 1942 the Board of Trade instructed many pits to close, but with much reduced staff the Headon works continued and took women on to their pay-roll. These were sometimes wives or sisters of the men who had gone to fight. Thanks to their efforts WBB continued throughout the war, still contributing to the economy of Cornwood and Lutton.

When peace returned all pits moved forward in production methods, with sophisticated modern machinery and an increasing amount of automation. Patterns of employment changed and clay workings, as with many other industries, had to operate with less manpower. The uses to which clay was put increased beyond imagination.

Little could William Cookworthy have dreamed that the clay he discovered would be produced 250 years later and be of such a high quality. He would be surprised that it is recognised as the best in the world and exported from the pits here in Cornwood Parish to all parts of the globe, pits where generations of Cornwood men have spent their working lives.

Above: *China clay workers (1930s?). Back row: seventh from left is Henry Stephens, eighth is Hodge (from Ivybridge), ninth and tenth are Eric Small and Bill Phillips. Front row: far left and third from left are Fred Small and Frank Small, fourth from left is George Greep, fifth, sixth and seventh are Walter Turner, Reg Maddick and Alf Cox.*

Left: *A page from the day book at Headon clayworks, dated 1914 and indicating the workers who were present on the dates between the 17th and 21st December. Regular workers would be paid an hourly rate, but others who 'bargained' would be paid so much per fathom of clay quarried, the price bargained for depending upon the difficulty of the ground. Turpin and Smerdon quarried 23 fathoms at 4 shillings per fathom over 11 days and earned £4.12s. Willcocks, Roberts, Mills and Phillips bargained for 40 fathoms at 3 shillings, which they completed in under six days and thereafter earned 3s.6d per day up to the eleventh day. Whereas these four men earned just over three pounds each in eleven days, Turpin and Smerdon earned only £2.6s, whilst the hourly-rate labourers earned £2.5s over the same period. Christmas Day fell on a Friday during the eleven days and was the only day not worked other than Sundays.*

Two rare photographs of women working in the clay pits during the 1940s, when the men labourers had been called up to the services. The top picture shows Edna Brown (left) and Dorothy (Belle) Stoneman at Headon clay-works and the lower picture shows Dorothy and Edna emptying a wagon. Their dress indicates that the work was cold and onerous but it was the fact that women proved themselves capable of such work that opened the door to a new era in which women established themselves as equals in the workplace.

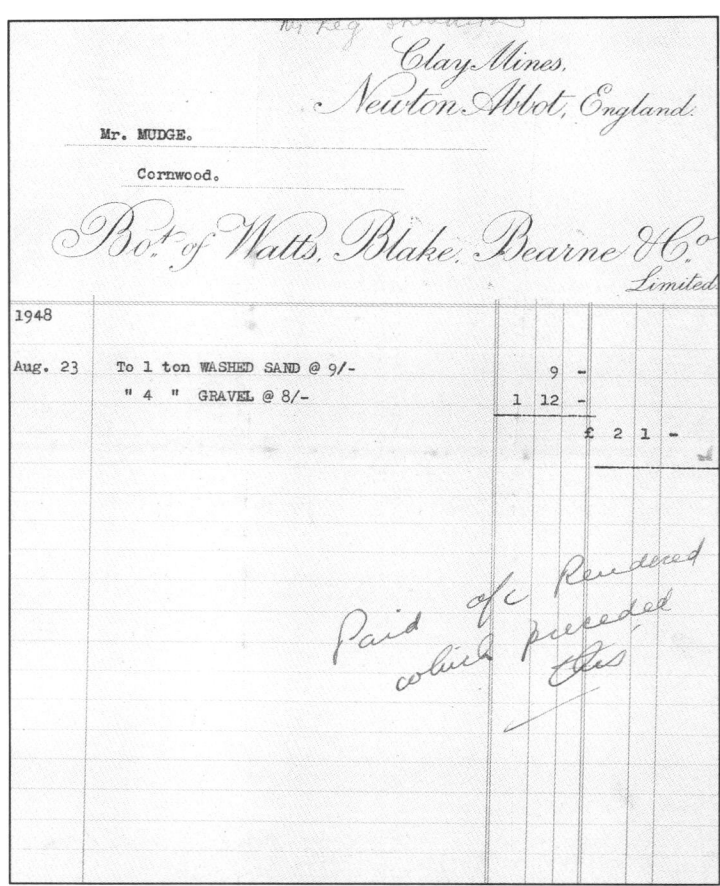

Above: *Alarm clocks were issued to clay-workers during the war years. This clock is in a black papier maché case and was imported from America.*

Right: *a receipt for sand and gravel, 1948.*

China clay pensioners and guests on an outing to Cornwall Clay Works where they met Prince Charles in 1969. Left to right - back row: 1. unknown; 2. Clem Roberts; 3. Fernley Cox; 4. Edna German; 5. Alvin Rendle. Front row: 1. Bob McNeil; 2. Maggie Roberts; 3. Margaret McNeil; 4. Mrs Sam Quest; 6. Nell Rendle.

Serving the Villages

To travel away from the villages was an adventure and not the necessity it can be today. If it can be said that at the heart of a community are the suppliers of goods, its shops, inns, post offices, and the people involved, then Cornwood and Lutton villages have had a sound heart for many generations.

From the middle of the 19th century we know that there were victuallers and innkeepers, shopkeepers. butchers, bakers, tailors and boot and shoemakers, all plying their trade within the villages, while blacksmiths, saddlers and wheelwrights enabled farmers and many others to carry on their work and leisure pursuits.

As transport changed from horse, cart and carriage to automobiles, so the wheelwright moved with the times, and became a garage, with petrol pumps to supply the traveller. Cars eventually became commonplace.

John Ford and Robert Mudge Snr. worked as wheewrights from the mid 1800s, followed by Robert Mudge Jnr and then Samuel Mudge, until, on his death in 1913, the business was taken over by William Stacey.

He was a very skilled man turning his hand to many crafts - wheelwright, signwriter, carpenter, and the undertaking business, not only the practical application, but supporting and dealing sympathetically with the bereaved. He ran a good workshop, employing men and teaching apprentices.

Automobiles started to be seen around the countryside, and in the late 1920s Mr Stacey installed petrol pumps. They were just under £100 each, hand operated, with the left one needing to be wound up, and the right hand pumped to and fro. Along with Colonel Parker of Delamore, and Mr George Green, headmaster of Cornwood School, he owned one of the first three cars in Cornwood. His first was a landaulette, with brass lamps, which his daughter Mrs May Poynter can remember having to polish until they shone, especially when there was a wedding or important occasion. This vehicle was used as a taxi, and although the passengers were under cover, the driver had a roof over his head, but no sides to the cab. This car, as with the following

The building with the rounded roof, once the paint shop when Mr Stacey made carts, became the garage for cars.

two, were bought from Miss Morris, of Nirvana, Ivybridge. She was fond of travelling on the continent, chauffeur driven, and when she changed her vehicle Mr Stacey had the opportunity to buy the previous one. His big cars would be hired to take families to Paignton, or Cornwall for the day, and he ran a taxi service, meeting trains at Cornwood Station.

The Stacey family were also one of the first to own a telephone - Cornwood 2 - number one being the Post Office.

In 1956 fire broke out in Mr Stacey's workshop, when tools and timber was destroyed. The building was afterwards developed as a cottage. Later the garage was owned by Mr Ivor Treby, who specialised in the little Fiat 500, and when national petrol companies supplied the larger garages only, the petrol pumps disappeared.

By 1985 the garage closed, and the building is now two private homes, one being called Wheelwright's Cottage.

Cornwood village wheelwright, Bond Street possibly taken before the Great War. Mr Stacey lived here from 1913 until 1959. In the photograph from left to right are: Mrs Stacey, her daughter May (now Mrs May Poynter), Harold Short, Arch Reglar, Dick Mills and Mr W.G. Stacey.

Mrs and Mrs W.G. Stacey and May Stacey, September 1935.

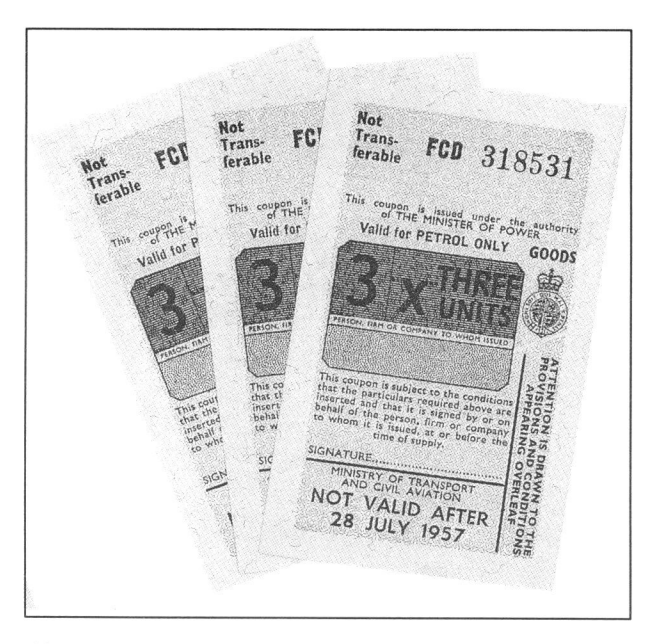

Above: *Petrol coupons. Fuel remained on ration until well after the war ended in 1945.*

PROPRIETOR   I.C. TREBY

CORNWOOD GARAGE

Servicing, engine and body repairs, welding & etc. Estimate free.

Lubricants, paraffin accessory store.

Fiat 500 & 126 specialists

Right: *Advertisement for Cornwood Garage, 1960s.*

Below: *Lutton too has had a garage over the years known, as ownership changed, as Lutton Garage, John Skelley, and The Astra Centre.*

The Old Smithy

From the latter part of the 19th century until after World War I, Francis Gray worked in Cornwood Square as the village blacksmith. The mounting block still remains and where anvil and furnace might once have been, today the workshop garages a 'Fergie' tractor.

The cottage adjoining is called 'The Smithy', reminding the passer-by of what took place there many years ago.

During the same period Thomas Kerswell and then William Lillicrap were also working as blacksmiths, but at Moor Cross.

Left: *Cornwood Square 1905 with the blacksmith Francis Gray. The boy is Frank Gray.*

Below: *A splendid Ferguson T20 tractor now has its home in the Old Smithy.*

The Butcher, the Baker, the Candlestick Maker...

In Cornwood there have been butchers and bakers, shoemakers and saddlers, ironmongers and shopkeepers of goods of many kinds, all down the years, and though the goods change, the welcome and opportunity to meet others while picking up a loaf of bread or newspaper is still there.

The present shop building has been a boot and shoemakers, and a saddlers shop, and now with a new window and the door moved round to the front, it becomes The Village Store. The building behind has also been a shop, but is now a private dwelling, called Saddlers Cottage.

Names change with the change of ownership - Perry's Store, Saddlers Shop, Ye Olde Shoppe, The Village Store, but everyday needs are found within no matter what the name above the door. Mrs Shepherd once kept a general store in Fore Street, where she sold many items, from sweets to wool, but to the youngsters walking home from school the latter items were the more important. Mrs Shepherd was very particular and kept her counter spotless; Olive Jeffery recalls one of the young customers, leaning forward to view the treats available, while Mrs Shepherd admonished 'Take your hands off the counter. I've just done it.'

Above: *The Village Store has seen a variety of uses during its long history.*

Right: *Moor Cross Cottages. In 1850 John Sandover, butcher, ran the Butchers' Arms Inn, and lived here. In 1889 they were occupied by Henry Vivian, carpenter, and Thomas Kerswell, blacksmith. In 1926 William Lillicrap, blacksmith, lived here.*

Top: *William Horton, a butcher in the 1920s and 30s, lived in one of Rose Cottages, Bond Street. The entrance was at the side, and in his front room he held a stock of sweets, like a 'Tuck Shop' especially for the young customers who would visit him after school. There were sherbet dips and lollypops, jelly babies and liquorice wheels, aniseed balls and sherbet fountains, and all at a price to suit the pupils from Cornwood School.*

Above: *Also in Bond Street, Wood Cottage was once a butchers with a slaughterhouse at the back. Mr Northmore supplied the meat and his wife sold milk and cream at her front door.*

Right: *Two receipts from the days when everything was supplied locally, from newspapers to FYM (farmyard manure!).*

The Village Inns

INNS

Tavistock Inn
1850 - James Doddridge

Butchers' Arms Moor Cross
1850 - John Sandover

Cornwood Inn
1866 - William Vivian
1878 - Walter Glover
1889 - John Glover
1897 - John Glover
1910 - John H Glover
1914 - John H Glover
1926 - William T Sandover
1939 - William H Sandover

Mountain Inn, Lutton
1878 - William Sanders
1889 - William Sanders
1897 - John Sanders
1910 - William F Lock
1914 - William F Lock
1926 - William John Balkwell
1939 - Wallace John Balkwell

From *Kelly's Directory'*

*Above right: The Mountain Inn,
Lutton as it was early this century
and retaining its old charm today.*

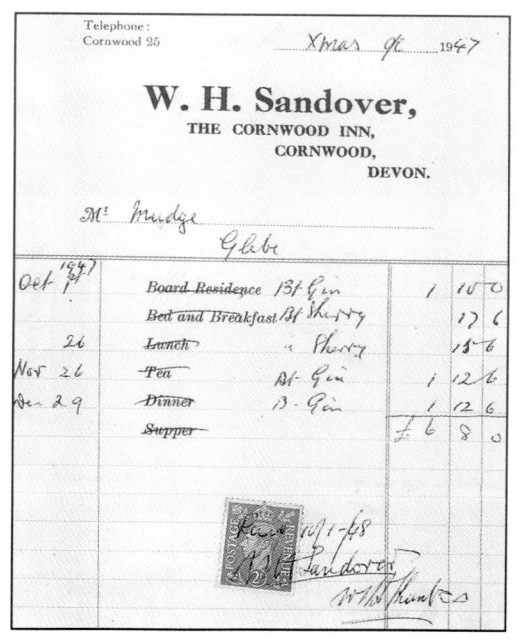

*Above and right: The Cornwood Inn today would be recognis-
able by those who used it 150 years ago, although the receipt
from 1947 reminds us how prices have changed.*

The Bakery

Wyn Jonas recalls an early bakery was run by the Vivian family who also ran the Post Office at the house that stands by itself in Fore Street, near the Old Clergy Cottages.

In time larger premises were needed and Mr Vivian built a house further along Fore Street with the bakery behind. The bakery round included Lee Moor, Lutton, the village and all the country farms and houses.

The Post Office was in one of the front rooms and also the telephone exchange. Florence Vivian handled all the calls.

The Vivian family were well known in Cornwood as shopkeepers and retailers, as well as bakers and Mrs E. Haynes remembers that after the baking was done, locals were allowed to put their own dough in the still hot oven.

The house owned by the Vivian family, now called the Old Bakery

The Post Office

Memories of the early Post Office also come from Wyn Jonas:

'When Mr and Mrs Richard Vivian retired in 1968, we took over the Post Office, moved it to Bond Street and ran it with the shop.

The post would arrive about 6.30am and there were two postmen who used to sort the mail, and at Christmas my kitchen was littered with mail as it was sorted for post on Christmas Eve. We took telegrams which my husband delivered, or other people if he wasn't around. Mrs Hambly, the post lady, would do her rounds, which included Slade and Lutton, on a bicycle.

In the early days we would open the shop on Sundays for the walkers who came by bus, and went to Hawns and Dendles, and would call in again for refreshment on their way home to catch the five o'clock bus.

The telephone kiosk was moved to where it is now the post box was put into the wall in our shop. One of my jobs was to clean the telephone kiosk everyday - the old red type then. We had an iron grill at the counter and we also supplied a clock for people to see the time. People would sometimes open the door just to see the time, much to my annoyance if I was busy doing some chores in the kitchen.

We enjoyed our time at the post office and stores. We were expected to be confidantes and advisers and of course we heard all the news. I still miss the retired gents who would come in for a daily chatter and tell us about their working days.'

The shop in Bond Street in 1959 before the Post Office was moved there. Patricia Jonas is filling the gum machine and the two lads are her brother Mervyn and his friend John Wragg.

The Post Office in Bond Street in the 1970s.

The earliest Post Office in Cornwood is thought to have been at what is now No.3 Bond Street. It was in the home of Mrs Northmore and her daughter Ann. Even today, by the side of the right hand doorway, the pointing between the granite blocks shows where the post box once was. The metal casing was found in the wall during renovation.

Before the end of the 19th century Albert Vivian was carrying on the family's long-established bakery and in the early 1900s he also became the sub-postmaster. His obituary was carried in the South Devon Times, July 1952.

FIFTY YEARS AT POST-OFFICE

Death of Mr. A. Vivian at Cornwood

Eighty-two years old Mr. Albert Vivian, who has been sub-post-master at Cornwood for over 50 years, has died after a short illness.

Mr. Vivian carried on his family's long established baking business for most of his life. He was a senior trustee of the Wakeham's Rooke Charity and for half a century was a sidesman at Cornwood parish church.

The Postmaster-General personally congratulated Mr. Vivian last year on his long service as sub-postmaster and his twenty-five years as manager of the local telephone exchange.

Post Office, Cornwood.

Left: *A postcard sent from Cornwood in 1909. Note the Cornwood postmark on the card, below.*

LUTTON

The cottages on the left are Gills Cottages, Lutton, where Phyllis Skelley ran a Post Office in her front room for nine years. She retired in 1970 and, as there was an existing Post Office within three miles, the Head Postmaster would not allow another to be opened.

Above: *Above: In some letterboxes in the parish, like this one at Moor Cross, the post may get eaten if left there overnight. The culprit - snails who love the taste of glue on the envelopes!*

Right: *1 Springfield Villas, New Road, Lutton, 1997. The house where Mrs Tall, always known as Aunty Gwen, ran a post Office from her front room.*

Various other people ran the Post Office after Mr and Mrs Jonas retired, and then in 1995 a new Post Office was built opening on to the Square. This was much safer for the public than walking down narrow Bond Street.

The new Post Office run by Ginny West carries a wide variety of goods for everyday needs, and offers the service of a dry cleaning agency, and shoe repairing among other things. The Post Office has tea rooms to offer refreshment to local people and visitors alike.

Cornwood and District Co-operative Society

Clifford Small recalls the days of the Cornwood Co-op: 'I was born in Rose Cottage in the village of Lutton in 1925, and moved with my parents to number 3 Newtown, Cornwood, in 1927. I started at the village church school when I was four, in 1929 and left 10 years later in 1939.

I joined the staff of the Cornwood and District Co-operative Society, though known locally as the Lutton Co-op, in the spring of 1940, looking after grocery and provisions.

The manager was Mr Lewis Standon Youldon. In the shop itself the first-hand was Mr Harry Tope, with assistants Mr Les Walters and myself. Our baker was George Nettison and our delivery man was Ernie Littlejohn who was responsible for delivering bread, buns, pasties and all the other things that might come out of our bakery. He was also responsible for delivering all our grocery orders, and they were many. The top yard was the butcher's shop, and our butcher, George Fuller. We also had a coal and paraffin delivery, done by Cecil Brooks, who in all winds and weathers delivered coal and coke to the housewife with much dependability.

In my day at Lutton, grocery and provisions was a trade and those of us who were engaged in it took a certain amount of pride in being able to do the job and do it well. There was an art in serving a customer. They'd always come once, but you wanted to see them again and again. In addition there were many things, in those days that came to the shop in bulk and these things had to be weighed and there was an art in knowing the different qualities of your currants, sultanas and raisins, and a host of other things as well. Currants, I remember, we used to weigh up on a Thursday afternoon, being the quietest time. They always went in blue bags and the sultanas went in golden, or amber bags. They had to be weighed and weighed precisely. The manager would quite often take a packet off the shelf and check its weight, and look out if it was wrong. There was an art in wrapping them also.

Up the stairs was our china department. There we sold cups and saucers, plates and tea pots - you name it, we sold it. Also upstairs was our drapery room. That's where we stored and sold sheets and pillowslips. The sheets were bleached and unbleached, and twill. In the next room we kept all our boots and shoes, adults and childrens. The alternative was a ten mile ride into the centre of Plymouth, plus the bus fare there and back again, so some things sold pretty well - men's chrome-leather boots for work, nailed and toe capped, and

The Co-op sold everything from soap to sideboards. This is a bill from 1946.

of course shiny leather boots for Sundays. We kept a fair stock of ladies shoes as well.

At the top of the stairs there was a large cupboard absolutely full from top to bottom of what I am going to call lamp glasses - lamp chimneys I think is their proper name - single burners, double burners, Aladdin lamps and all the host of others. On the right was our mat room. The front room was full of saucepans and kettles, and mixing bowls.

Looking at the front of the shop there were two large windows, with mirrors at the back. There was a large doorway, with two doors, and if you went inside and looked carefully, on the door that didn't open often, there was a very stout strong iron bar. At one time the shop was broken into, so when we finished our work at night we shut the doors, slipped the bolts up and dropped the bolt down into place and it was locked. There were iron bars on the glass windows so that made it just about burglar-proof.

The shop - quite a large one for a village store - had two counters. The one on the right was used for serving customers and in the centre of it, were the scales, because so many things had to be weighed. On the other side the counter was used for putting up orders. The cash till was there, and the bacon machine, and my word it was sharp!

There were goods in that shop from floor to ceiling and there were shelves all the way round. Behind the serving counter we endeavoured to keep those things that were in greatest demand. We kept our currants, sultanas and raisins there, and margarine; in those days that was only used for cooking. There were three qualities - purple seal, red seal and silver seal, according to the colour of the wrapper, but what a delightful price! Purple seal, 5d a pound (old money), red seal 7d and silver seal 9d a pound. We kept our tea and our coffee there - cheap tea 6d a quarter and the very best tea, number 23 or 99 (and they are still sold by the Co-op today), 9d a quarter.

There were two shelves absolutely full of jams and marmalade. The best selling jam was the mixture of strawberry and gooseberry. You could tell a person's income by the quality of the jam they bought. If a lot of money didn't go into the house it was plum jam, and if a better income it might even be strawberry on its own. And there were sauces and pickles and so on.

There was no chemist for miles, so we kept aspros and aspirins, cough mixtures - very popular in the winter - and Owbridges Lung Tonic and teething powders for babies. You name it and we tried to sell it.

On the other side, behind the till there were two shelves that were absolutely full of breakfast cereals and another shelf all the way round full of tinned fruit, those for Sunday tea. On the top shelf we stored goods sometimes medicines, that did not deteriorate with keeping. I remember liquid paraffin was a pretty good seller.

At the inside end of the customer counter was a marble slab and on the right of that slab we kept the lard. Lard came in 28lb blocks, and you weighed it up on a sheet of greaseproof paper, and with the lard knife the art was to cut a piece that weighed accurately - 4oz or 8 oz or 1 lb. A good grocer would reckon to get it pretty well perfect every time!

On the other side, a little way away from the lard, was the cheese box of the cheese machine. It was a box with a very strong wire for cutting the cheese, and we prided ourselves on selling a good quality cheese - a lot of men took it to work. In those days the best quality Cheddar was 6d a lb!

The manager had a little downstairs office, with a desk and chair, and there were mirrors with which he could see pretty well all round the shop. When he was there we were never idle!

In the yard we had a back store and here we had goods that didn't mix over eagerly with grocery. There were various cleaners, and our loose vinegar in a barrel. We kept there the things that came in by the sackful as many things did in those days, and at the far end on a platform, we kept our flour. The flour was weighed for us by the baker in the bakery, with a white paper bag containing 3.5lbs and a craft brown bag contained 7lbs.

We used to purchase our salt by the truck load as it was that much cheaper. Some huge bars weighed about 28lbs for when a farmer killed a pig and salted it, they needed a lot of salt and the Co-op was there to sell it.

All the baker's flour came by the truck load, delivered by the railway, and it was stored where it was warm and dry above the bakery. We also kept what we called forage, barley meal and the cheap one called 'sharps', for the housewife who couldn't afford good quality barley meal for her hens. It was a few coppers cheaper for 7lbs. There was also maize and wheat and oats kept in large bins. The corn was emptied into the bins and one of them contained mixed corn.

During the wartime if a housewife kept a few hens in her garden she had to forfeit her egg coupons, and in their place she got vouchers which entitled her to buy meal for her fowls.

Opening times were 8.30am, closed for lunch at 1pm and open for the afternoon from 2pm to 6pm. Whilst I was there 6pm became 5.30pm and Saturday closing became 12.30pm instead of 1pm, and what a difference that made to us especially if we wanted to catch the bus to Plymouth which went just after one.

Fundamental to the Co-operatve Society were the shareholders. Anyone could be a shareholder and the share cost £1. The average householder allowed her dividend to accumulate until she got her £1 share, and once she got that, she could collect the dividends if she wished. Very often the housewife would take and use her dividend money to buy a pair of sheets for the bed or a new pair of boots for her husband, and although the 'mickey' was taken out of the Co-op and its 'divi' there was many a youngster who went to school with a new pair of shoes or boots because they were paid for out of the 'divi'.

That establishment was very dear to my heart. It wasn't all that long ago that folks put up enough capital to get it built. In the early days I believe it came under Bristol, until it had enough capital to be independent, but as long as that shop was there, with its groceries, its coal, its paraffin, its butchery department and its fresh bread every day, it was the heart of the community and the heart of the villages.'

The Village Policeman

The policeman lived in Havelock Terrace, Lutton, a house that had Devon Constabulary over the door, and later it was at Copper's End, Corntown. 'Although the policeman would frighten the life out of you, you could talk to him, when all's said and done,' recalls Mrs Doris Baskerville.

Mrs E Doddridge of Gibb Hill remembered that there was an earlier Police House (before Havelock Terrace) down New Road. The policeman then lived in Chapel Cottages and his name was Constable Reglar These cottages were demolished before Sept.1984.

Above: *The police house at Havelock Terrace, Lutton.*

Coppers End, Corntown.

Electricity

'I remember, and I am sure there will be many others who remember, when electricity came to Cornwood,' recalls Clifford Small. 'But it came to Lutton much earlier, the late 1930s I think. It was the war that prevented the necessary work being done to bring it further. In the first place there had to be sufficient homes willing to have it installed to make it viable. A survey was taken and there were more homes requiring the power in Lutton than in Cornwood. At a meeting of the Parish Council, Mr Harry Tope (Lutton) made a statement. "What Lutton does today, Cornwood does tomorrow". The *South Devon Times* reported on the meeting and used this comment as a headline and you can imagine the result!

After the war, when the load in many homes was increased, with electric cookers being the main culprit, on Sunday mornings, there was frequently a power failure. At the Chapel this would be obvious to us when the organ was switched on for the final hymn. No organ also meant no hot Sunday lunch, indeed it happened to us on our first married Sunday!

The Board would do little about it until a friend loaned me a volt meter and readings were taken over a period proving that at times the voltage was about half what it ought to have been. Then, and not before, was the requisite improvement made. (and they never did ask who loaned me the meter!).

It was with envious eyes that from Cornwood we looked across to Lutton, after the war, and saw the roads lit up and realised the cost was included in our rates and we were in darkness still!'

LETTER TO THE EDITOR

No Electricity Yet at Cornwood

To the Editor "South Devon Times"

Sir—The harvest is past, the summer is ended, and we at Cornwood are still without electricity. Why?

Yes, yes, I know that, ten years ago or more, half the people turned it down. But, surely, that's no reason why, in 1949, A.D., no visible steps seem to be taken to give the long over-due supply?

Of course, we have our battery for the radio, the hub dynamo for the bike, and candle for the hall. But, what about the electric lighting and cooker, fire, washer, iron, and the host of other electrically-powered appliances?

We at Cornwood do not expect a round-about at Bus Style or an Oxford Circus at the end of Bond Street. But, for crying out loud, give us electricity NOW!

BERTRAM F. SMALL.
24, Newtown,
Cornwood.
Sept. 22, 1949.

Notes from the diary of Mrs Dorothy Cox.
ELECTRICITY

Church House was wired for electric light on Monday May 22nd to May 25th 1950 and the lights were switched on June 15th 1950.

The electric cooker was installed on 29th October 1953.

The electric street lights were switched on in Cornwood 13th February 1951 and in Newtown on the 14th.

Wakehams Rooke had electricity switched on indoors on 11th December 1958 and in the outbuildings the next day.

Water

Most outlying farms and houses had their own water supplies from springs, and many still do. The villages had to rely on communal water supplies that were provided originally from springs or leats, and later from wells, often with a hand pump used to draw the water from the ground. The 'common water taps' came into general use about a hundred years ago and are still dotted around the parish. Barbara Green remembers one being two steps down, between Wood Cottage and the Post Office in Bond Street.

The water tap in Yondertown Square, 1985 (since rebuilt).

The village well in Fore Street, Cornwood in 1884. The girl fetching water was Phyllis Haynes who lived in Bay Cottage, about 100 yards from the well. The building in the background is the Cornwood Inn.

The Library

Lanthorn House and Club House. There was a library held in the Club Rooms in Bond Street, run by the WI. It was Id for members and 2d for non-members per book taken out. All the books were covered in brown paper covers to keep them clean, and these had to be replaced regularly.

Today the mobile library from Ivybridge visits Lutton and Cornwood regularly.

There was once a small lending library run in the Legion Hall, Lutton. This is now a private house.

Grandfer Roberts, Bill Turpin's father and friend take a well-earned rest on Langham Levels after walking to Ivybridge, c. 1910.

These days the Community Bus takes people to Ivybridge.

Getting Around

Up to the early years of the present century people seldom travelled far from their homes. Travellers in country regions would complain, on asking for directions, that the locals had no idea where roads led to. Road signs were non-existent or were simple crosses and milestones carved with the initial letter of the next village en route.

Horses were used by some but walking was the main mode of getting about the place and even the bicycle, when it became commonplace elsewhere, was not so popular in hilly Devon.

In the 1900s motor transport was only for the rich and before that the wealthy employed the horse and carriage to convey them about the country. It was not until the 1950s that most working men and women could afford to own a car, although the motorcycle became popular much earlier, especially for young men.

The two photographs below illustrate the use of carriages by the gentry. The horse has played an important role in the village, both as an individual mount and in teams pulling carriages, wagons and farm machinery. There are still many stable buildings to be found, for example, Prettypool House, which, according to its present owner, was once home to the Delamore estate bailiff.

Above: Admiral Parker (second row) and friends crossing the river at Two Bridges, about thirteen miles from Cornwood in 1899. They were on their way to a meet of the Dartmoor Hunt.

Left: The marriage of the carriage, horse and railway. Henry, with horses Miller and Totnes, waiting with the Delamore carriage for passengers at Cornwood station, 10 April 1890.

China clay was taken to the railway station by horse and cart. Harry Sharp says that, probably about 1920, his grandfather, Richard Colton, would take his cart with a team of two horses to the clay works and haul the company's clay. No doubt others did the same, and to this day hauliers are contracted to use their lorries to haul clay from Headon works by lorry.

Over the years the quantity of material produced, the size of the lorries and the frequency of their journeys has increased. The road to the south of Langham bridge was widened and the curves reduced in severity to reduce congestion. The road from Langham bridge northward, however, through Cornwood village to the Heathfield is still narrow. Modern lorries fill the whole width of the road near The Square and there is a real danger that pedestrians on the pavement could be accidentally injured by a passing lorry, no matter how carefully driven. It is impossible to pass in places and reversing and queuing traffic became commonplace. But the villagers wanted to keep their narrow road because it both kept its character and reduced traffic speeds. Pressure to exclude heavy vehicies grew over the years and the clay quarry owners eventually agreed to route long distance traffic away from the village in the 1980s Householders on the route feared that vibrations from the increasingly heavy short-haul lorries would affect their buildings; parents feared for the safety of their young children. In 1997, after many years of pressure, the highway authorities finally excluded heavy vehicles from the parish if they were only passing through.

Basil Stephens of 3 Bond Street, demonstrates two modes of transport, above in 1927, and right in 1930s.

Reg Snowden on his Sunbeam motorbike, before the First World War.

A report from the South Devon Times, *July 1952.*

There are numerous footpaths and bridleways in the parish marking routes and shortcuts important to people in their daily lives. Paths link places such as East Rooke and West Rooke farms; Lutton and Slade. Other routes were droveways along which farmers took their cattle to grazing on the moor.

Muriel Bloomfield remembers having to walk from Lutton to Cornwood twice a day to school: "The roads were extremely rough. They were made up with layers of small stones and chippings and then covered with liquid tar which smelt horrible. It was then rolled with a steam-roller, which caused quite a bit of excitement. There were sites at various places where large pieces of stone were stacked, and these were broken down by a man with a hammer."

After the second World War coaches also brought people into the village. Mrs. E.M. Haynes remembers coach parties coming to Wisdome Bridge and Hawns and Dendles. Groups from Plymouth enjoying parties in the Cornwood Inn garden on Wednesdays and Saturdays are recalled.

The bus service to Plymouth has always been important, with up to a dozen journeys each way. By 1997 these had dwindled to half as many, reflecting the increasing use of the car. The last bus from Plymouth, 9.00p.m., would probably have allowed people to see a film show in the days when performances were continuous.

Charabanc outlings to the coast and to the moors were tremendously popular during the 1920s and 30s. This photograph shows 'Close Harmony', the Lutton Congregational Sunday School's outing to Paignton in 1924. There were usually six or seven charabancs. 1. ?; 2. Mrs Sercombe (Florrie's mother); 3-5. ?; 6. Mr Harry Skelley; 7. Mrs Sercombe (Dorothy's mother); 8. Dorothy Sercombe; 9. Mr Sercombe (Dorothy's father); 10. Olive Sowden; 11-13. ?; 14. William Roberts; 15-16. ?; 17. Mr Jack Blackshaw Snr; 18. ?; 19. Jack Blackshaw Jnr; 20-21. ?; 22. Edwin Luscombe; 23. Mrs Millie Luscombe (mother of Edwin and Arnold); 24 Arnold Luscombe; 25. ?; 26. Mrs Doddridge (aunt of Muriel): 27. Muriel Roberts: 28. Mrs Emily Skelley: 29. ?; 30. Mrs Sowden (mother of Olive): 31. Mrs Sowden's son (either Reg, George or Lewis); 32-34. ?; 35. The driver; 36. Stanley Stancombe.

An outing from Cornwood and Lutton to Torbay and Paignton, 1926. The man in the centre in the trilby is Mr Balkwill. The second lady on his left is Mrs Lucy Burnett, the little girl is Eileen Phillips, with her mother, Mary Phillips, next to her. In front of them, with her arm over the side, is Miss Gwen Yelland. Others present on the outing include Mr and Mrs Bert Shepherd, Miss Marjorie Phillips, Miss Beatrice Haynes, Mr Cyril Bowden, Mr and Mrs Frank Bowden, and Miss Nellie Reglar. The driver was from J Hoarce and Son of Ivybridge.

Left: William Skelley, of Lutton, and Arthur Lee of Lee Mill. They swept the Lee Mill lanes together, but Mr Skelley alone swept Cornwood Square.

Bridges

The parish has many rivers and streams gathering water from the moor. Some of the crossing places are very ancient and narrow bridges survive from packhorse days. This is Vicarage bridge, taken in 1876.

The Railway

According to E.T MacDermott in his *History of the Great Western Railway*, the South Devon Railway, later to become part of the Great Western Railway, opened the line from Totnes to Laira on 5 May 1848. It was a single track line of the 7ft broad gauge. In 1852 Cornwood station was opened.

Cornwood Notes (1918) declared: 'Cornwood owes a great debt of gratitude to Sir Isambard Brunel, the famous Engineer, who brought the South Devon Railway through the parish, spanning its valleys with lofty viaducts, instead of using the less hilly route to the South. This modest railway, with its single line narrow gauge, was afterwards absorbed by the more important Great Western Railway, and a more substantial viaduct took the place of the old one, wide enough to allow a double line of broad gauge.

All this was a great advantage, for with a Station within easy reach of the village, the inhabitants were brought into closer touch with their neighbours and the outer world, and enabled them to obtain commodities, not to say the necessities of life, in a quicker and more convenient manner.

The Railway, however, has not added to the picturesqueness of the parish, since it has brought slate to it from the Cornish and Welsh quarries, which have taken the place of the thatch that covered many of the cottages in former years. No longer does the sweet aroma of the peat fires greet one, but its fragrance has been supplanted by the smoke and fumes of coal and petroleum, and there is perhaps only one house in the parish following the ancient practice of burning peat, though more as a luxury than a necessity.'

The railway converted to the present narrow gauge in 1892. *Cornwood and Lutton Magazine* reported in June: 'The conversion of the broad into the narrow gauge was accomplished with wonderful success on Saturday May 21st.

Temperance people, and still more those who are not so, may take notice that this feat has been done without the aid of beer or other stimulants.

6,000 men worked 16 hours a day, on a work of special hardness and urgency, and they did it on Oatmeal Drink and not alchohol! Beer, spirits etc. (as beverages) are a useless luxury; and no one who wastes his money on them can be considered a poor man.

MacDermot tells us that only 4200 men were used. Gangs of about 20 men each dealt with about a mile of track. The company supplied the oatmeal for the drink, but the men supplied their own food. Elsewhere these navvies had a formidable reputation for drunkeness.

A train crosses Slade viaduct in this nineteenth century engraving. Designed by Brunel, with stone piers and timber spans, it was 273 yards long and almost 100 feet high. Blachford viaduct was of similar construction.

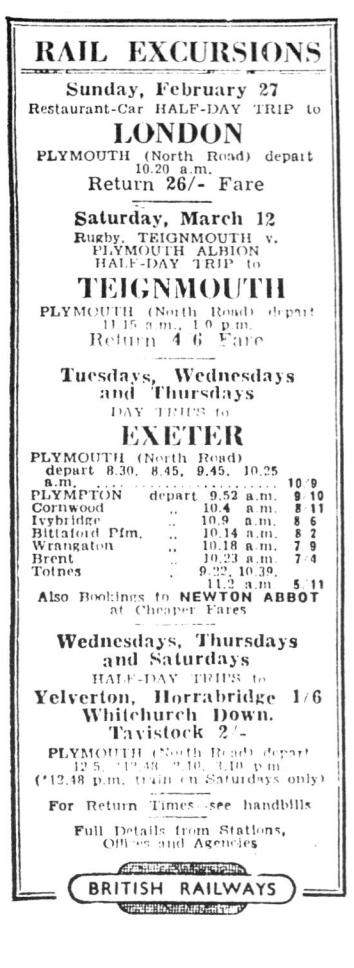

Above: *The old piers of the original viaduct stand alongside the existing arches of Slade viaduct.*

Right: *A newspaper advertisement for rail excursions in 1949. Direct journeys from Cornwood to all places mentioned, except Plymouth and Plympton, can now only be made by car. A community bus makes one journey a week to Ivybridge, while a Plymouth supermarket provides free transport for shoppers once a week.*

Below: *Thomas Phillips won the 'Best Kept Station' award in the early 1900s. Signalman Charlie Winsor helps to tend the flowerbeds.*

THE RAILWAY

The railway was also used for day trips. Here is a humorous report from a newspaper item *Cornwood Crumbs* 22 August 1898

'The peaceful slumbers of the inhabitants of the villages of Sparkwell, Lutton and Cornwood, were disturbed very early the other morning by the rumbling of wheels, cracking of the whip, and the sound of voices talking. One individual dresses himself and prepares for another day's toil, thinking there may be an eclipse of the sun. But with the dawn of day comes the news. Poor Cornwood Church Choir party have been stuck in the mud. It was decided to train to Plymouth and go up the river to Calstock, stopping at Pentillie for a couple of hours.

But, it was not to be, for on nearing Pentillie there they were, stuck in the mud, and could no further go. Mustn't it have been lively. But the worst was to come, for on reaching Millbay Station to return home to their surprise the last train had gone, and the vicar had to hire brakes to take the party home. When they arrived it was in the small hours of the morning.

The choir seem to have forgotten their adventures on the Tamar as this report from the *Cornwood Parish Magazine* of August 1928 indicates.

'We left Cornwood Station, a party of 37, at 9.36am on Saturday July 14th, for Exmouth. The splendid weather with which we began continued with us through out the day and materially added to the general enjoyment. The journey by steamer from Starcross to Exmouth was on such a day delightful. On reaching our goal we made immediately for Emery's Cafe, where wraps, hats, etc. were discarded, and each and all went their respective ways until 4.30, when we reassembled and sat down to an excellent tea, to which full justice was done The party then broke up again and made for the sea-front, from which it was not easy for them to drag themselves away so as to meet again at the Cafe at 7.5 to catch the 7.30 boat for the last train to Cornwood, which we reached at 10.15 - half-an-hour late - after a most happy and enjoyable time, in recognition of which we "render thanks to the Giver", on the Station platform, by singing the Doxology. '

Left: *Cornwood station in the early 1900s. The station was important for villagers as it was the only direct link to Ivybridge. There was a siding for the despatch of china clay.*
Below left: *A locomotive at Cornwood station, 1900.*
Below right: *Station House in 1988. The windows with the extended porch are typical of the style adopted by South Devon Railway.*

Just to the north of the Church of St Michael and All Angels, and overlooking the churchyard is Church House. Today it is a private residence, and has been so for many years, but it was built in 1818 as a small Dame school - some say for orphans - with living accommodation upstairs for the schoolmistress. It is believed that the garden of the next door house provided the playground, and at one time, according to Kelly's Directory, *the teacher was Mrs Mary Ann Northmore.*

By the time that John Duke Pode and his son Cyril Augustin Pode compiled Cornwood Notes *in 1918, its use as a school had long gone, and meetings of the Church Council had been held there, and Cornwood had new large school buildings erected in the village.*

Below: *Cornwood School, 1890. The school had a bell tower at that time, and the schoolmaster lived in the School House at the near end of the building.*

Cornwood Schooldays

Cornwood School was at one time known as the Cornwood National School and today is Cornwood Church of England Primary School. On the front of the substantial Victorian building in School Lane, Cornwood are inscribed three mottoes in Latin:

FIDELI CERTA MERCES
Reward is certain for him that keeps faith.

NOS NOSTRAQUE DEO
We dedicate to God ourselves and all we have.

NEC PRAEDA NEC PRAEDO
I shall be neither robbed nor robber.

In 1859 a school for the children of Cornwood was built on land where Bays farmhouse had once stood, and at the Fore Street end of the school was the house for the schoolmaster.

On 13 August, 1859 The *London Illustrated News* reported: "New School at Cornwood, South Devon: This school, recently opened, was erected principally at the cost of Lady Rogers of Blachford, on a site given by Mrs Praed of Delamore. On the opening day the Rev. F. W. Gray conducted service at Cornwood Church, before a crowded congregation.

The children afterwards, to the number of nearly one hundred and fifty, were regaled with tea and presented with suitable books by Sir Frederick Rogers, Bart. Later in the day the whole company attended in the beautiful grounds at the back of Blachford, where games amongst the children terminated the evening. The building, nearly one hundred feet in length, has been erected from designs by Mr Alfred Norman, of Devonport, architect, and comprise a large schoolroom, with a classroom, with bell turret at the east end, and a master's house at the west end. The walls are of granite of varied colour, from the neighbouring moors. The chimneys and sides and heads of the windows are of beautiful grey and cream coloured firebricks, the gift of the Earl of Morley. They are from the china clay works at Blackalder, in the neighbouring parish of Shaw, which have been developed and brought to their present perfection by Mr Phillips, the energetic and successful manager."

On 2 June, 1861 the school inspector reported:

"These beautiful school buildings are an ornament to the parish, and are complete in every way". But he goes on to say: "The discipline is not yet steady enough, but instruction in reading, writing and needlework has made good progress. In arithmetic great improvement must be looked for."

So Cornwood children had their school, and it stands today looking much as it did well over a hundred years ago. What changes has the building seen?

Today two new classrooms stand behind the old building and what at one time provided two rooms, divided by a wood partition with glass in the upper part, is now a hall with many uses. The infant classroom in the rounded end once had a bell tower above it, and the room had a gallery. According to the school log book the tower was still in place in the 1920s, though reported to have defects, but by 1910 the gallery had been removed as being unsafe.

But the old school would feel that today the children are cared for and taught as they always have been since Septimus Green became the headmaster in 1874. Of the earlier staff little is known apart from names: Mr Hill, Mr Hocken, but it appears that Mr Green gave a great deal to Cornwood and Cornwood children. From accounts written at the time of his death in 1925 he was a loving and much loved man. He was a schoolmaster, poet, organist and choirmaster and played a full part in village life. He helped to establish a young men's club and the Cornwood Brass Band, and even ran an Evening School for lads on Mondays, Wednesdays and Fridays, so that they "might not forget nearly all they ever knew."

In his day and that of his son George Green, who took over as headmaster when his father retired, it wasn't all work and no play. There were games in the Hams followed by teas, and annual treats including boating on Blachford lake. The children were given a monthly half day holiday as a reward for good attendance (this features frequently in the school log books) and had half days for the Cottage Garden Show, and Empire Day, and a whole day on account of the Cornwood Show, which it seems was held on a weekday, and also a day for the Lutton Sunday School Outing.

Cornwood School in the 1890s. The top picture shows the Schoolmaster, Septimus Green, with the boys' class, the lower picture is the girls and mixed infants with Mrs Sarah Green (née Deveson), or possibly Miss Rowe.

Cornwood School c. 1910. The little girl in the front is Ruby Cox and the tall girl at the back, right hand side, is Annie Cox. Other pupils are: Violet Mudge; Eva Churchward; Ida Turpin; Carrie Horton; Queenie Champ; Rosa Mills; Rhoda Mudge; Elsie Kelly; Marion Endicott; Ruby Corber; Cassie Pascoe; Ethel Lock; Alice Horton; Lily Geake; Alice Hillson; Muriel Bowden; Dolly Short; Lynn Horton; May Venner; W. Stephens; T. Baskerville. Surnames only are known for: Kelly; Mills; Searle; Willcocks; and Sercombe.

Cornwood School, 1911. The Schoolmaster at this time was George Green and the teacher on the right is thought to be Miss Dustin Hannaford. Attending the school in 1911 were: Mary and Reginald Hosgood; Frances and Henry Vivian; Margaret and Fernley Cox; Edward and Victoria Champ; Olive and Florence Green; Clare and Frank Horton; Charles and John Munford; Alfred and Kate Hillson; George and John Endacott; Percy, Edith and Violet Mudge; Florence Smerdon; Wallace Pascoe; Eric Baker; Samuel Burnett; Frances Ede; Ernest Hext; Hetty Northmore; Enid Phillips; Elsie Kelly; Fred Westward; John Skidmore; John Glover; Dora Churchward; Harold Short; Frances Gray; Ellen Reglar.

The *Parish Magazine* of January 1911 gave details of dressmaking at the school. "The Devon Education Committee have written to say that Miss B.W. Smith will give 12 weekly lessons at 3.30 pm, in the Club Room, by kind permission of Miss Deare. Will intending students send in their names to the Vicar *at once*? I have four names already. The first names sent in will be selected. The following memo should be noted from head-quarters: 12 students can join the practical class, others may look on as spectators. Preference should be given to those over 16, and to those able to attend every lesson, as they are progressive, one growing out of the other. Students provide their own material, and may make dresses for themselves or others, provided that the latter come to be measured and fitted. Information and advice as to quantity and quality of materials to get will be given by the Instructress at the first lesson. To the first lesson students should bring measuring tape, pencil, pins, and a paper skirt pattern of Weldon's or some penny paper."

Two views of school classes in 1911. In the top photograph the teacher is Sarah Green, wife of Septimus Green. From left: Back row: 9. Fernley Cox: Middle row: 5. Annie Cox: Front row: 9. Jack Munford: 10 Bill Greep. On her retirement from Cornwood School in 1913, after twenty years, she was presented with a silver teapot, hotwater jug, sugar basin, cream jug and teaspoons by Miss Deare, who hoped that Mrs Green would long live to enjoy her retirement. She did, for she died in 1955 at the age of 106 years!

Cornwood School cookery Class, c. 1911. From left - back row: *Eva Churchward, Edie Hooper, Emma Skelley, Annie Ede, Violet Mudge.* Middle Row: *unknown, Olive Mills, Edie Mudge, Annie Cox, Emily Colton, Rosie Mills, Frances Ede.* Front row: *Beatie Davey; Dora Churchward, Carrie Horton.*

Cornwood School, early 1920s. From left - back row: *1. Evelyn Cox; 2. ?; 3. Jo Hext; 4. Frank Baskerville; 5. ?; 6. Clarence Skelley; 7. Billy Roberts; 8. Hubert Cox.* Middle row: *1. Arthur Wright; 2. Frank Broome; 3. Gwennie Daniels; 4. Elizabeth Mumford; 5. Ethel Mudge; 6. Emmy Skelley; 7. Ruth Horton; 8. Doris Hulson; 9. Norman Blackler.* Sitting: *1. Ethel Sowden; 2. George Hext; 3. Henry Tibbett; 4. Frank Sowden; 5. Lesley Sercombe; 6. Minnie Luscombe.*

Cornwood School, early 1920s. Left to right - back row: *1. Bessie Hillson; 2. Ivor Willcocks; 3. Roy Sercombe; 4. Phyllis Roberts; 5. Amy Baskerville; 6. Rosa Pawley; 7. Lilian Hosgood; 8. Harry Northmore; 9. Cyril Greep;* Middle row: *1. Marjorie Short; 2. Fred Roberts; 3. Freda Mills; 4. Hazel Willcocks; 5. Mabel Skidmore; 6. Ida Skidmore; 7. Gwennie Elliott; 8. Marjorie Hillson; 9. unknown.* Front row: *1. Connie Hosgood; 2. May Stacey; 3. unknown; 4. Florie Lillicrap; 5. Marjorie Searl; 6. Sid Steer.*

Cornwood School, late 1920s. From left - back row: *1. Edwin Luscombe; 2-3. unknown; 4. Geoffrey Roberts; 5 Jack Blackshaw; 6. Norman Willcocks; 7. Jack Wills; 8. unknwon.* Middle row: *1. Rosie Osborne; 2. Phil Blackler; 3. Harry Baskerville; 4. Gordon Rendle; 5. Clifford Cox; 6. Douglas Drew; 7. Bob Skelley; 8. George Wills; 9. Edward Balkwill; 10. Gerald Skelley; 11. Edna Balkwill.* Front row (sitting): *1. Eileen Phillips; 2. Barbara Drew; 3-4. unknown; 5. Phyllis Haynes; 6. May Rundle.* Front row (kneeling): *1. Ida Roberts 2-3. unknown; 4.Lorna Rendle.*

Cornwood School, late 1920s - The teacher pictured is Mr Channing and the Headmaster at the time was Mr George Bishop. From left - back row: 1. George Wills; 2. John Warley; 3. Jim Amos; 4-7 unknown; 8. Phil Blackler; 9. Bob Skelley. Middle row: 1. Jack Blackshaw; 2. Geoff Roberts; 3. unknown; 4. Rosie Osborne; 5. Blanche Luscombe; 7. Joan Rendle; 8. Mary Horton; 9. Peggy Downing; 10-11 unknown. Front row (sitting): 1. unknown; 2. Phyllis Haynes; 3. Edna Balkwill; 4. unknown; 5. Ida Roberts; 6. May Rundle; 7. Dorothy Hillson; (kneeling): 1. unknown; 2. Jack Wills; 3. Norman Willcocks.

Cornwood School, late 1920s. From left - back row: 8. Norman Willcocks; 9. Gerald Skelley. Middle row: 4. Phil Blackler; 6. Clifford Cox; 7. Douglas Drew; 10. Robert Skelley; 12. May Rundle. Front row: 1. Dorothy Hillson; 2. Phyllis Haynes; 6. Eileen Phillips. Other names are unknown.

Cornwood School, Infants, 1926. Teacher Miss Ellen Reglar. From left - back row: 2. ? Small; 4. Clifford Cox; 5. Harry Baskerville; 7. Geoff Roberts; 8. Douglas Drew; 9. George Wills. Middle row: 1. Edna Balkwill; 3. Rosie Osbome ; 5. Mary Horton. Front row (sitting on form): 3. Dorothy Hillson; 4. Phyllis Haynes; 5. Ruth Cudlip; 6. Betty Collins; 7. Alec Luscombe; Front row (sitting on ground): 4. Jack Blackshaw.

Cornwood School, about 1930. From left - back row: 1. Ken Downing; 2. Peter Armstrong; 3. Len Drew; 4. Len Tidball; 5. Alistair Roberts; 6. Cyril Phillips; 7. Cyril Mudge; 8. Claude Amos; 9. Fred Willcocks. Middle row: 1. John Pryce; 2. Peggy Murphy; 6. Angela Hitchens; 7. Phyllis Greenslade; 8. Peggy Downing; 10. Kathleen Phillips; 11. Nancy Locke; 12. Frank Osborne. Front row (kneeling): 1. Barbara Rowe; 2. Marion Willcocks; 3. Violet Phillips; 4. Rosalie Whitford; 5. Phyllis Skelley; 6. Joyce Rendle; 7. Barbara Willcocks; 9. Tina Willcocks; 10. Pat Ham; (sitting): 1. Charlie Rendle; 2. Clifford Skelley; 3. Basil Stephens; 5. Alf Kingwell; 6. Ronald Phillips; 7. Sam Phillips; 8. Walter Rundle.

CORNWOOD SCHOOLDAYS

THERE ARE SOME ENTRIES IN THE SCHOOL LOG BOOKS THAT CATCH THE EYE:

3.10.1907.   Caned several children who came late to school in the afternoon, having stopped up at the church to witness a wedding, although warned by the Buttwoman at the time.

24.3.1910.   Miss A E Green left Cornwood School after over twenty years, and has been appointed mistress at Lutton School.

9.5.1910.   School opened with singing of National Anthem for King George V owing to the lamentable death of King Edward VII.

13.7.1910.   Afternoon session commenced at 1.30pm to admit of children carrying the men's teas to the harvest fields.

18.10.1910.   Very wet afternoon - several children got wet through going home to dinner. Five children who had changed and returned from long distances and were less than five minutes late, had their absence marks cancelled. (more than five minutes late brought punishment).

18.12.1914.   The teachers and girls have knitted for soldiers and sailors at the front - 12 pairs of mittens: 10 pairs of socks; 8 sleeping caps: 9 scarves; 11 body belts and 2 girdles.

14.5.1917.   After Prayers spoke to the children on the need for food economy, as desired by Lord Davenport. and also of the need for going to bed early, in accordance with instructions received.

1.10.1918.   Morning devoted to blackberry picking, in accordance with government instructions.

11.11.1918.   Shortly after assembly I heard the sirens and hooters of Plymouth sounding loud and prolonged blasts. I made the necessary preparations for hoisting the flag, as I anticipated that they signified the acceptance by Germany of the Allied terms for an armistice. It was not until 9.30am that I could obtain confirmation by telephonic communication from Plymouth.

Cornwood School, c. 1930. From left - back row: 1. Alistair Roberts; 2. Cyril Mudge; 3. Frank Osborne; 4. Lewis Skidmore; 5. Edward Balkwill; 6. Frank Skelley; 7. John Pryce; 8. Clifford Skelley; 9. Charlie Rendle; 10. Peter Arrnstrong. Middle row: 1. Gerald Skelley; 2. Peggy Downing; 4. Phyllis Greenslade; 5. Gordon Rendle; 6. Clifford Cox; 7. Douglas Drew; 8. Harry Baskerville; 9. Lorna Rendle; 10. Ruth Cudlip; Front row: 1. Tina Willcocks; 3. Eva Collins; 4. Barbara Rowe; 5. Kathleen Phillips; 6. Barbara Drew; 7. Pat Ham.

In 1927 the school served an area of over ten and a half square miles with a population of some 1,100 and with no other school in the area. There are many parents and grandparents of the children at the school now who spent their childhood at Cornwood School. and have memories of those times and the teachers who taught them.

Mr Channing first came to Cornwood as an Assistant Master in 1929 (when the Headteacher was Mr George Bishop), and left at the end of 1937, returning in March 1944 as Headteacher, having this appointment until 1970. Many children have passed through his hands, and many will remember his contribution to the village.

In April 1948, in accordance with the 1944 Education Act, Cornwood School was reorganised and became a Primary School. As reported in the School Log Book, "Previously the school had been 'All Age', and at the close of the Spring Term 1948. there were eighty-five children on roll. All 11+ pupils were transferred at the opening of the Summer Term to Plympton Secondary Modern School".

The school opened on 12 April 1948 with 55 children on Roll. As this was below the '60' grade, the school now became a "Two Teacher School" necessitating considerable change in organisation. Miss H. A. Ryder took over Infants and Juniors, and the Head Teacher took 7 to 11+.

In 1959 Mr Channing saw the Centenary of the School, and in August 1968 the school had a playing field, thanks to the generous co-operation of Major F. G. W. Parker.

Pat den Hollander remembers: "Mr Channing always carried a cane by his side and he kept it on his desk. You could hear a pin drop in his classroom. He was always keen to talk on current affairs, and inspired an interest in the children. When we had some spare time we were allowed to look at his copies of the *National Geographic* magazine - quite a treat!"

During the war Mr Lawley took over the headship of the school. In the School Log Book for 11.9.1939 it was recorded that there were many children from a school in Acton, London evacuated to Cornwood. and as the building would not accommodate them all, the Cornwood children should use the school building from 9am to 12 noon and the Acton children, with their teachers, would be there from 1.30 to 4.30pm. When not in the school the children were taking their lessons in the Public Hall.

Mr Len Copley came as Headmaster in 1976. He was a very keen walker on the moors and led groups of people in the parish when Beating the Bounds.

Miss Florence Gwyther was Assistant Teacher with the infants from 1930 to 1941 and by all accounts she was very much loved by the small children in her care.

Miss Hannah Ryder, another Assistant Teacher, was also a favourite with her pupils. She then lived in Ivybridge and in the early days caught the train to Cornwood. The school then had one hundred and fifty pupils with ages from five to fourteen. When the trains became unreliable she would cycle to work. Today Bert Small remembers how "Miss Ryder had a sort of small oven over the coke stove in her room, and she used to warm the children's pies ready for lunch."

She once said "I think that a child's first day at school must be an awe-inspiring ordeal, walking into a schoolroom and being confronted with hordes of strange children. My aim is to make them feel at home, and I try to mix kindness with firmness." When she retired in 1962 , after almost forty-two years in the school, there were donations from a total of one hundred and twenty-one people, including parents and friends. There were many of her 'old pupils' who could not be at the retirement ceremony, and a tape-recording was played containing messages from them. She was remembered with great affection.

And now Cornwood Primary School has a Headteacher, Mrs Sue Pritchard-Jenkins, appointed in May 1991.

Cornwood School by Luthfi Gulliver

Cornwood School 1932-3. Schoolmistress, Miss Florence Gwyther. From left - back row: 1. Sam Phillips; 2. Jack Blackshaw; 3. Reg Murphy; 4. Fred Willcocks; 5. Len Drew; 6. Basil Stephens; 7. Jack Phillips; 8. Peter Armstrong; 9. Alf Kingwell; 10. Ken Downing; 11. Walter Rundle; 12. Marjorie Blackler (monitor). Middle row: 1. Rosalie Whitford; 2. Lucy Willcocks; 3. Phyllis Murphy; 4. Marjorie Riches; 5. Kathleen Hooper; 6. Molly Moger; 7. Irene Prouse; 8. Nancy Locke; 9. Eva Warley; 10 Marion Willcocks; 11. Eileen Rundle; Front row: 1. Jack Bradley; 2. Phyllis Skelley; 3. Barbara Willcocks; 4. Hilda Cudlip; 5. Violet Phillips; 6. Cynthia Downing; 8. Joyce Rendle; 9. Morris Mojer.

Cornwood School 1991. Headteacher Mrs Sue Pritchard-Jenkins. From left - back row: 1. Lee Ansell; 2. Stacey Cousins. Long row: 1. Nicholas Hutchins; 2. Carrie Renshaw; 3. Rachel Smith; 4. Rachel Briggs; 5. Mark Austin; 6. Scott Jones; 7. James Horgan; 8. Christian Dearing. Centre: 1. Jenny Walters; 2. Lyndsey Reed; 3. Anna Bawn; far right hand side, Shaun Turpin. Front row: 1. David Honey; 2. Mrs Pritchard-Jenkins; 3. Karen Ednie (half hidden); Adele Fowler; Gemma Skidmore. Sitting on ground: 1. Abby Jago; 2. Sarah-Jane Sharman; 3. Shelley Honey.

Cornwood School Football Team - 1910-1911. From Left - back row: *1. Ern Rendle; 2. Harold Elford; 3. Bill Colton; 5. Frank Gray; 6. Mr George Green.* Middle row: *1. Alvin Rendle; 2. Walter Turner; 3. John Endacott; 4. Jack Skidmore.* Front row: *1. Sam Burnett; 2. Frank Horton; 3. Charlie Locke.*

Cornwood School Football Team - 1993. From left - back row: *1. Mark Symons; 2. Wayne Randle; 3. Christopher Pyne; 5. Chris Briggs; 6. David Hurn; 7. Jack Quest.* Front row: *1. Mark Stallard; 2. Shane Harper; 3. James Turpin; 4. Jonathan Lomas; 5. Kevin Hurn.*

Schools in Lutton

From the memories of local people it seems that the first school in Lutton was at 1, Myrtle Cottages. It was a Dame School, but no further information has come to light.

1 Myrtle Cottages, Lutton.

The Reverend Duke Yonge gave land at Lutton, together with a sum of money, so that the Trustees of the Yonge Charity could apply the income for the benefit of the poor of the parish of Cornwood. One part was directed to the education of a certain number of poor children of the parish, selected by the Vicar, and to the teaching of the catechism and principles of the Church of England.

From the *Cornwood Notes* we learn that in 1875 a small schoolroom for infants was built at Lutton by some of the landowners of the parish, on land belonging to the Yonge Charity Trust - the birth of Lutton School. Later an addition was made by Admiral Parker in the form of a chancel and vestry, so that Divine Service could be held there on Sunday afternoons.

From a letter written in October 1884, it seems that a house was needed for the schoolmistress, (the lady there at that time was to retire and she lived in a cottage nearby). Lord Blachford had a house built in 1885, on land belonging to the Charity and Mrs Packer took over the teaching at the school.

The *Cornwood Parish Magazine* of March 1892 records that "the Managers have abolished School Fees at Lutton, for the relief of parents, although no compensation for them will be received from the Government. It gives no grant at all for Lutton School." The report goes on to say that the H.M.Inspectors find the children in good order and the instruction continues to be efficient.

And again in January 1912 it is reported that "Lutton is a small school of infants, yet one in which good work is being done. The children knew their Bibles very well and did their teacher credit and were eager to answer. Those deserving honourable mention were Reginald Sowden, Kate Hillson, Herbert Skidmore, Norman Blackler, John Baskerville, Harry Blackler and George Sowden." Lack of money did not hinder good results!

The *Cornwood Parish Magazine* made mention that "On 16th October 1902 the presentation of a purse containing £11.15s, contributed to by 162 subscribers, was made by Admiral Parker to Mrs Packer on her resigning the post of Infant Mistress at Lutton Church School after eighteen years service."

As the school was for Infants only the children from Lutton moved on to the Cornwood School as they became old enough. By 1923 the school closed, and all Lutton children attended Cornwood School, often walking the distance four times a day as they returned home for a mid-day meal.

Between 1975 and 1987 the school building and the house were sold, as the Charity found it impossible to maintain the buildings.

The school is now a private dwelling called Pallion, and the high ceiling of the main room shows its origins, while the schoolmistress' house retains its link with the past as it is still called School House.

School House, Lutton, today. Now a private house.

Lutton Infant School, 1921. Run by the Church of England - Teacher Mrs Blampey. From left - back row: 1. Mrs Blampey; 2. Olive Sowden; 3. Gladys Blackler; 4. Doris Sowden; 5. Norah Sedgeman; 6. Ethel Small. Middle row: 1. Marjorie Blackler; 2. Frances Shepherd; 3. Charlie Mudge; 4. ? Johnson; 5. John Balkwill; 6. Edna Roberts; 7. Robert Rendle; 8. Frances Skelley; 9. Fred Roberts; 10. Florrie Sercombe; Little girl in centre - Joyce Roberts. Front row: 1. Winnie Wilcox; 2. Jack Osborne; 3. Alec Luscombe; 4. Alvin Mudge; 5 Ned

The Cornwood and Lutton Under Fives Group continues the tradition of education in the parish for the very young. Here, in 1993, children meet the Devon Fire and Rescue Service mascot, the Wellyphant.

From left - back row:
1. Emma Barker; 2. Heather Palmer; 3. Oliver Cook; 4. Nicola Melling; 5. Katie Pearce; 6. Elizabeth Style; 7. Tim Horton; 8. Ashley Delooze; 9. Robert Atkins; 10. Samantha Greep; 11. Jenny Hamlyn; 12. Tom Howard; 13. Alex Rouse. Front row: 1. James Butlin-Jones; 2. Alice Hurn; 3. Jamie Munton; 4. Damiel Moore; 5. Chloe Jarvis; 6. Ryan Bewes.

People and Places

Blatchford

In 1085-6 Domesday records two manors of Blacheurde (now Blachford) in the Hundred of Ermington. This is confirmed in the early tax returns (Feudal Aids) of 1302-3. One was then called Over Blachworthy (the present Blachford), which appears to have been centred on the hamlet of Tor and covered the area Hall Cross - Yadsworthy - High House and south to the glebe of Cornwood, but it does not appear to have extended west of the Yealm lower down. Nether Blachworthy appears to have by then become the glebe.

The oldest part of the house now standing at Blachford appears to date from the sixteenth century, but the earliest date recorded is on a lintel on a barn - 'IH. VH. 1627' - which was when the manor was owned by the Heles. They were a numerous and at one time wealthy family in the area and began to build a house alongside the old farmhouse at Wisdome in 1627. At that time they appear to have owned Higher and Lower Hele and to have lived in the latter.

In 1690 John Rogers, a former customs man, who appears to have made a fortune as a merchant - some say in tobacco and others pilchards - bought the estate of Wisdome and the lordship of the manor of North (Over) Blachworthy from John Hele. Included in the purchase were ten hogsheads of cider, four great moorstone troughs and the right to pasture on Stealdon Moor. From then on he was known as John Rogers of Wisdome.

In the next ten years John Rogers established himself in the protestant world which had grown up after the Glorious Revolution of 1688. His ambition may have been fired by the fact that he was a descendent of John Rogers who was the first protestant martyr to be burnt at Smithfield in 1555. His own father, a Fifth Monarchy puritan, had been imprisoned in Cromwell's time and John's brother was born in prison.

As a king's man Rogers progressed rapidly, buying the Manor of Ivybridge in 1692 and the Manors of Blachford, apart from some rights retained by the Heles, two years later. In 1698 he was elected MP for Plymouth and the following year was created baronet on payment of £1095 to the Crown to maintain a troop of foot in the garrison of Ireland for three years.

In 1698 he gave his son John his interest in the manors of Ivybridge and Blachford on his marriage. John then went to live at Blachford while his father remained at Wisdome where he raised twelve children.

Five years after the death of the first Sir John, his son acquired the reversion of the remaining leasehold property at Blachford from Thomas Hele. This man was to prove an embarrassment for on 28 June 1723 he appeared before him in the manorial court and admitted 'tipling' until midnight at the inn at Tor kept by the widowed Mrs Elizabeth Woodward. On a second occasion Thomas appeared on a charge of thrusting a burning brand in her face during a 'disagreement'.

The second Sir John remodelled the house at Blachford in the early eighteenth century. He and his heirs continued to play a leading role in the area as MPs and Recorders for Plymouth. The third Sir John became High Sheriff of the county of Devon. His wife was the Dame Hannah who founded the orphanage in Plymouth which later moved to Ivybridge and now is run by the Spastics Society. She had no children herself and the estate passed to Sir John's brother, a captain in the Royal Navy, in 1773.

Sir Frederick Leman Rogers became the fifth baronet in 1777, having eloped with 16-year-old Jenny Lillicrap to Gretna Green eight years before. He is best known for building the first Church of England chapel in Ivybridge and for running a successful racecourse on Hanger Down.

The lake in front of the house was built in 1827 by Sir John Leman Rogers, the sixth baronet, and the house was again modernised in his time. His brother Sir Frederick who had in 1810 married Miss Sophia Deare became seventh baronet. He left his entire estate to his wife and it was Dame Sophia who after his death in 1851 began energetically to develop it. Money was provided for a school and parsonage in Ivybridge, and land and money for a school in Cornwood. In 1856 Blachford properties at Lutton, Corntown and Cross were exchanged for Delamore land and for the houses which John Bond, a wheelwright, had built in about 1820 in Bond Street, with three cottages at Puddepool. In 1864 she got perrmission to close the old road from Cross through Blachford grounds to Hall Cross and to make the road to Harford the one via Vicarage Bridge.

It was the eldest son of Dame Sophia who was made Baron Blachford of Wisdome in 1871. He continued his mother's tradition of public works, enabling Dame Hannah Rogers school to move to Ivybridge, building the reading room at Lutton and doing much for St Michael's Church. After he died the cross in the square in Cornwood was erected in his memory.

Lord and Lady Blachford had no children so the title died out and the baronetcy passed successively to two of Lord Blachford's brothers, both unmarried, until with the death of Rev. Sir Edward Rogers in 1895 the baronetcy also died out. The estate was inherited eventually in 1900 by the Misses Louisa and Margaret Deare. After the death of her sister, the latter was for some years a dominant figure in the village. In 1917 she passed most of the Blachford estate, and shortly after the Manor of Ivybridge, to Major Frederick Passy whose wife was her cousin. Miss Margaret Deare left Blachford in 1925 to live in London, after passing to Major Passy the remainder of the estate, the house and the deer park.

Fountain memorial to Louisa Deare at Blachford.

On his death in 1955 the whole estate passed to Wing-Commander Cyril Passy and in 1971, by now much reduced in size, it was inherited by his widow Jennifer. She died in 1983 and Blachford was sold at auction two years later to Sir John

Major Frederick Passy at Blachford, c. 1951

Greenaway from Kent. In 1986 it was bought by Mr Paul West who has carried out extensive rebuilding and modernisation of the old part of the house in particular.

During the time of Miss Deare at Blachford, between 1900 and 1918, the estate consisted of some 20 farms, many of them small by present standards. It was largely self-supporting since apart from the produce of the farms it had its own mills, sawmill and two sand quarries at Hanger and Gorage Waste.

Apart from wood from the estate, turf was cut on the moor, carted down and dried for use as peat. There was an outside staff of twenty, including the steward, Mr Shepherd, the keeper, stone-mason, carpenters, cowman, woodmen, carter, coachman and handymen. The inside staff of about eight were under the butler.

Miss Deare rode round parts of the estate regularly - the way was through a series of the characteristic 'ball' gates. At first she rode on horseback and later in her carriage, usually with a cock pheasant's feather sticking up from the bridle between the horse's ears. She was sometimes to be seen in the village walking with a stick and accompanied by her lady's maid, Miss Wardell. As well as being president of the Working Men's Club which met in the house in Bond Street (Lanthorns), built by Lord Blachford originally for the men who worked on the Slade viaduct, she was also in charge of the Sunday School. This was taken by Mrs Lindesay who marched the children from Cornwood School to church at 10.45 on a Sunday.

On Ascension Day the Blachford staff had to go to church. Those children at the school who went to church on that day had a half-day afterwards. Methodists and others worked at school all day.

During the summer holiday the school was invited to Blachford for a picnic and the children were taken on the lake in two rowing boats.

Most of what we know about the early history of Blachford is due to the work of Mr Charles Hankin of Ivybridge who over many years has catalogued the Passy Papers in the West Devon Record Office with the permission of the family. This note is based on Charles Hankin's work which he has kindly made available.

Far left: *Miss Deare at Blachford with groom, George Crimp.* Left: *Florence Irene 'Queenie' Gosling, who lived and worked at Blachford, 1941.* Below left: *Grandad Frank Greep giving trap rides c. 1949-50. The boy is Mervyn Baskerville, the little girl Ann German and the girl sitting is Sheila Baskerville.* Below: *Lewis Baker, 1949, gamekeeper at Blachford. He lived at Hanger Villa.*

Above: *Blachford sawmill which supplied all the timber for the estate, from a drawing by Richard Rose-Casemore.*

Right: *George Crimp, groom, with everyday trap.*

Below: *Paul West, Geoff Fox and terrier, Cindy, in the Marathon Cart drawn by Duke and Prince outside Blachford, 1997.*

Delamore

In the beautiful valleys below Penn Beacon men have lived since the earliest days. From the 13th century onwards records exist to show that a number of important families began to settle in the area and among the houses mentioned were Slade, Fardel, Blachford and Delamore.

Three Lords of the Manor, Cornwood, Corntown, and Lutton are entailed on Delamore which, post Domesday, belonged successively to the families of Roddon, Bothe and Metsted. Later, about the middle of the 14th century, the Courtenays possessed it until the attainder of the Marquis of Exeter. Later still the Manor with the mansion of Dallamoor, belonged to the Cole family who were also owners of Slade. It was Cole who built the first Delamore House, next to the existing Home Farm.

It passed next to Robert Bellmaine whose tablet appears in Cornwood Church, and was then acquired by Sir George Treby of Langage Farm, Plympton in 1667. This was the last time that Delamore was bought and it has remained in the same family, sometimes through the distaff side, ever since. The Treby daughters (painted by Gainsborough and Reynolds) married Benjamin Hayes and Admiral Ourry respectively. The Hayes built the second Delamore on the Mount. Their daughter married Judge Praed whose only daughter in turn married the younger son of Sir William Parker (who was Nelson's Captain). The wedding gift was the present Delamore built in 1859 by J.P. St Aubyn. Admiral George Parker died in 1904 and was succeeded by his son Colonel William Parker (Rifle Brigade). His son Captain William 'Jo' Parker (Rifle Brigade) was killed in Flanders in 1915, aged 28, leaving Major F.A.V. Parker (Rifle Brigade) and Letitia Parker. Miss Parker married Major D.S. Dollard producing 2 sons, Christopher

(Rifle Brigade) and Gavin Dollard who presently lives in Cornwood. Mrs F.A.V. Parker still lives at Delamore.

The present house (listed Grade II) was originally heated by large conservatories at each end which, no doubt supplied so much for the beautifully laid out garden which, to this day, still contains many old rhododendrons. Of particular interest in the drawing-room is a large window, the upper part of which comprised eight etched glass panels, each 24x18 inches. They tell a story concerning one of the earlier Heles, one Sampson Hele of Fardel, who at the time of the Civil War was a zealous Royalist. He was with Prince Maurice at the siege of Plymouth. Depicted, is the Royalist Army on the march, the assault of the ramparts, and Sampson Hele himself who was sent to treat with the Parliamentarians and was held captive. They are attractive and unique.

Much of the Estate is laid out for hunting and shooting with many acres of forestry and open moor. Admiral Parker owned the Dartmoor hounds buying them outright from Charles Trelawney of Coldrennick in 1887. He hunted them for 13 years passing them on to his son-in-law William 'Squire' Coryton of Pentillie Castle on the Tamar. His grandson was also master between 1955-1962. Colonel Parker was Chairman of the Hunt and the family has been closely connected with the hunt ever since.

Another item of particular interest is the Chapel. This was built as part of the house and was converted to Roman Catholic Service by Major F.A.V. Parker in 1974.

At present Delamore is an agricultural estate with 7 farms, mixed forestry and several cottages spread over the two different parishes of Cornwood and Modbury.

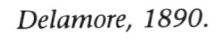

Delamore, 1890.

Above left: *Admiral Parker.*

Above: *Admiral Parker and Mackworth Parker on Charlie, photographed at Slade, 1875.*

Left: *Evelyn Parker and Mary Parker (right), 1875.*

Top left: *Robert Lang, labourer at Delamore, 1875. He and his wife, Jenny, were living at Delamore Farm in 1871.*
Top right: *Coachman's cottage and stables, Delamore, 1890.*
Above: *Delamore showing the chapel, 1876.*
Left: *Colonel Parker 1940-41, with his nurse Sylvia Oliver and her niece, Anne Riley, who stayed at Delamore during the war.*

Tea for tenants at Delamore on rent-paying day, 1905.

Fardel

Perhaps the most important historically of all the four manors of Cornwood, is Fardel Manor, between Cornwood and Ivybridge: a meticulously preserved and restored medieval mansion.

More history is available on Fardel than we have space for but the occupants can be traced back to before Domesday, with Romans, Saxons and Druids all involved! In the time of Henry III the property belonged to Warren Fitz Joell whose heiress brought it by marriage to Newton. By a later marriage with a Newton heiress it was acquired by Symond Ralegh of Smallridge. He was the grandfather of Sir Walter Ralegh whose father, Walter was born here and lived here for some time. In 1613 it was sold by Sir Carew Ralegh to Elizeus Hele who bequeathed it with other estates to charities and to Hele School Exeter. His right to do this was disputed by the heirs and it was retained by the family until 1740 when it was purchased by Thomas Pearse of Bigbury who 'kept a pack of hounds there' [Baring-Gould]. His executors sold it to Sir Robert Palk of Torquay, whose tenants John Butcher and Reeve Richard Sheperd farmed the land.

In 1844 it was divided into two portions between Sir John Rogers and Spurrell Pode, with the Podes living at Fardel. The last Pode to live there sold it in 1918 to Ray Cocks who sold it to John Ray in 1947. It was finally purchased by Dr Anthony Stevens in 1971.

Perhaps the most famous part of Fardel is the Fardel Stone. The Rev Samuel Pearse found it forming part of a culvert over the stream at the top of the drive. Only ten ancient inscribed stones have been found in Devon and only two bear Ogham characters (Fardell and Buckland Monachorum). It is now in the British Musuem and is described earlier in this book.

Between the house and the Ivybridge road lies a field which in olden times was the subject of much mystery. Tradition says that some untold evil would surely follow were it ever to be ploughed up; moreover it is related that ghostlike apparitions had been seen there in the dead of night. A doggerel couplet has been handed down which is quoted by Baring-Gould:

Between this stone and Fardel Hall,
Lies as much money as the Devil can haul.

As a result, we are informed, the field has never been ploughed!

Fardell was built in the form of a triangle, the house stretching across one end of it while the high garden walls completed the other two sides. The only windows were inside these walls over-looking the garden. The house has a projecting front porch commanding the sole entrance to the garden. The small room over the porch has windows on three sides to command the approach of a possible enemy. A curved ceiling in a small room upstairs near the porch showed (before 1945) that this was originally the minstrels' gallery of the Great hall, the upper part of which had been turned into bedrooms. The old open fireplace in the hall still remains. The main house has been extensively and beautifully restored by the present owner.

On passing through the fine granite piers of the gateway at the entrance to the Manor House, there is on the left a Chapel with its quaint south porch, bearing on it a small granite cross, similar to the one surmounting the east end of the roof. Facing you on entering the building are the remains of an ancient doorway leading into the road, from which it is evident that it was not merely a domestic Chapel, but was also used by the tenants and public. It is recorded in 1422 that licence for Divine Service was granted to Elizabeth Ralegh. Additionally the Chapel has a fine east window with granite mullions of the late 14th century period but there are signs of an earlier one, possibly of the 13th century. There are some interesting features in the south wall belonging to the earlier date, namely a Credence, Piscina and Dedile. More unusual is the Easter Sepulchre in the north wall, and at the west end there are the remains of the Aumvries, much dilapidated, one being in the north wall and the other opposite.

Of much more interest to modern historians was the re-use of the Chapel in 1965. A service was held in Fardel Chapel for the first time in two hundred years on 8th August 1965. The service replaced evensong at Cornwood Church and was part of efforts to raise money for the restoration fund. The service was taken by Rev. William Hamley and he and the choir walked in procession from the house to the crowded chapel with the main bell tolling. The procession was watched by some 400 people who visited the manor during the day.

The house is now owned and lived in by Dr Anthony Stevens and the land is farmed by Mr Dennis.

The western entrance to Fardel Manor, from a photograph taken in 1886.

Top left: *Fardel Manor, west porch in the late nineteenth century.*

Left: *West porch after the addition of a chimney.*

Above: *John Ray*

Below: *Fardel Manor - the south front today.*

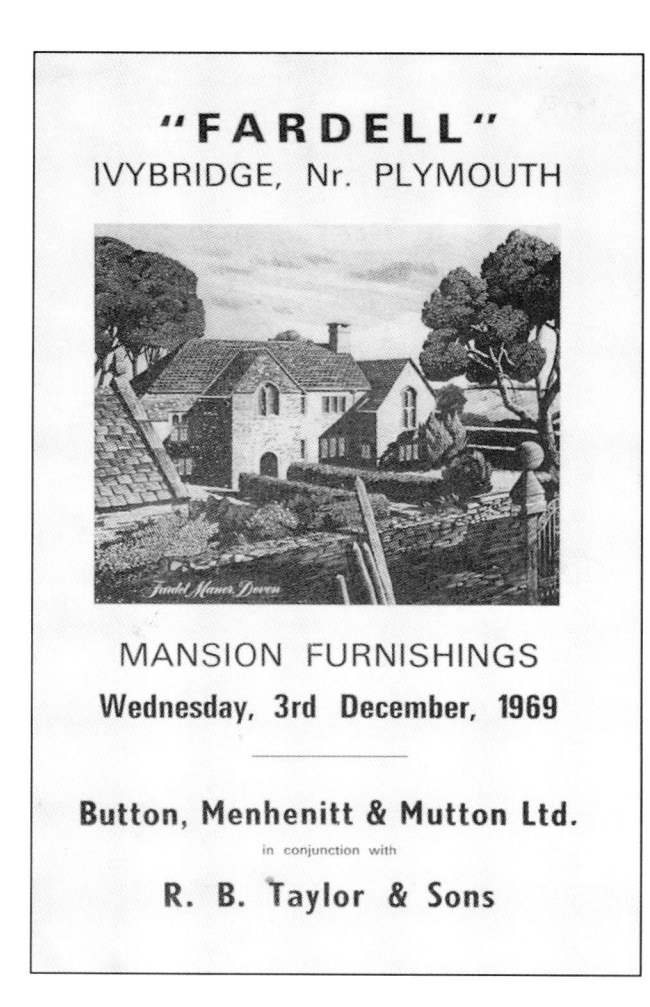

"FARDELL"
IVYBRIDGE, Nr. PLYMOUTH

MANSION FURNISHINGS
Wednesday, 3rd December, 1969

Button, Menhenitt & Mutton Ltd.
in conjunction with
R. B. Taylor & Sons

Above: *A view from the Banqueting Hall at Fardel looking through to the Great Hall.*
Left: *A handbill giving notice of the auction of furnishings from Fardel Manor in 1969.*

Above: *A detail from one of the Christmas Cards personally drawn by John Ray.*

Fardel Mill Farmhouse, July 1946.

Above: *Fardel chapel in the late 1950s.*

Left: *An open day in aid of the Parish Church Restoration Fund on Sunday 20 September 1967 was attended by hundreds of people and the service was relayed to the Water garden and the banquetting and Saxon halls for those unable to find seats in the chapel. From left: Olive Collum, Doris Pengelley, Minnie Steer, Vera Roberts, Mrs Davenport, Margaret Lang, Ida Skidmore and Olive Jeffery.*

Slade

In the early thirteenth century the first house on the site was built by Walter de la Slade and was known as Slade Hall. The hall itself within the house was completed in 1212. Much of the original house was burnt down in 1405 and re-built in 1415

When the Slade family died out the house was acquired by Reginald Cole in the time of Henry IV (1399-1413). He came from a large and ancient family - Sir Simon Cole was in the train of the Duke of Gloucester at Agincourt. Five generations of Coles lived at Slade until it was sold in 1610 and shortly after came into the possession of Cristofer Savery of Modbury, a member of a well connected family. The fortunes of this branch of the family declined in the eighteenth century and the house became dilapidated, eventually being sold by Waltham Savery in 1780 to John Spurrell, who later passed it on to his nephew John Pode of St Budeaux.

The Podes, who lived there for two hundred years, largely rebuilt the house in 1820. The last of the family to live at Slade was John Duke Pode, MA, JP. He was grandson of Rev. Duke Yonge and wrote *Cornwood Notes*, the first history of the parish. In 1911 he built Fitzworthy and lived there in his later years, finally selling Slade to Reginald Martin in 1922.

The Martins repaired the house - it had been empty for four years - but when in the year 1931 both his wife and their only son died, Reginald Martin and his daughter Nancy moved to Lee Moor House and Slade was let until 1957. Then Nancy and her husband Eric Hare bought the house from the family and made extensive repairs, demolishing the west wing. In the course of the repairs they found three old oak doors and a fresco of a saracen which they had framed. Before they moved there in 1959 the house was blessed room by room and sprinkled with holy water by Canon Edward Ward, Queen's Chaplain at Windsor.

Later, in 1980, the Hares went to live in Slade Barton having sold the house to Mrs Veryan Williams-Wynne.

In medieval times Slade owned a fishpond, a warren, mills and a trout stream, as well as gardens and woods. The great barn, measuring 180 feet by 56 feet, still stands with its granite doorway and there is a handsome stable block in which is a fine clock. In the gardens, which include a large walled kitchen garden, is an ancient hornbeam hedge said to have been planted in the time of Elizabeth I. At one time Slade owned 11 farms including Great and Little Stert, but all the farmland apart from 110 acres was sold by J.D. Pode.

Due to the rebuilding over nearly 800 years the house contains elements of the Tudor, late Jacobean and early and late Georgian periods. Fortunately the great medieval hall remains. It is open to the roof in which there are 60 carved bosses. The hall has intricately carved panels in relief and a minstrels' gallery.

Slade. A photograph taken c. 1850, not long after it was rebuilt by the Pode family.

Above: *Slade, from a drawing by Beatrice Pode, 1894.*

Left: *The Pode family, 1872. As John Duke Pode is not on any of the photographs in the family albums it can be assumed that he is the photographer. He was the son of Thomas Julian Pode, of Plympton Erie and Slade, and Anne Duke, daughter of the Rev. Duke Yonge, Vicar of Cornwood. His wife was Augusta Boevey Pode, daughter of the Rev. Charles Crawley. She died in 1900. Their eldest son, Ernest Duke Yonge Pode, died on the P&O SS Bokhara, when it was driven off its course by a typhoon and wrecked on rocks in the Straits between China and Formosa, in 1892. He was the medical officer. Their second son Cyril Augustin Pode became a War Department Land Agent. Arthur Crawley Pode their youngest son practised as a solicitor and they had one daughter, Beatrice Catharina Pode. Other relatives are Duke Yonge, C C Yonge, John Yonge, Charles Coleridge Pode, and (not in photograph above) Margaret Crawley .*

Left, below: *The Old Pound house at Slade, c. 1875.*

Above: *A view of the extensive kitchen garden at Slade from the barn, 1876, providing the estate with home-grown produce.*
Below: *A wonderfully evocative photograph of Beatrice Catharina Pode.*

Above: *Beatrice, Cyril, Arthur and 'Foscar'.*

Above: *The Great Barn at Slade, 1876.*

Far left: *Mrs Jackman at Slade in 1937. Her husband was gardener and they lived at Slade Lodge.*

Left: *Joan and John Osborne who lived at the Lodge between 1959 and 1968. He was groundsman for Major Hare at Slade.*

Left below: *Family transport in the late 1950s. Anne Blackshaw, Sandra Ashman, Shirley and Muriel Osborne and John Osborne's motorcycle and sidecar.*

Hanger

Hanger has a very long history, certainly dating back to the 12th century. Hanger and Cholwichtown are the two oldest farms in the parish. Although many changes have taken place the basic shape is still that of a Devon Longhouse. The family lived at one end and the animals at the downslope end, with an entrance and passageway giving access to both.

For nearly 300 years Hanger had been an independent freeholding owned by the Fortescues. In 1892 it became part of the Manor of Blachford until, in 1962, it once again became an independent freeholding.

In 1965 the new owners gave considerable thought and effort trying to unravel the changes that had taken place over hundreds of years. It was found that the past generations, who had made Hanger their home, had each left their mark. Although many questions remain unanswered, the property, as it is today, shows the very best in the natural development of English architecture.

Above: *Hanger today.* Right: *Doorway from the main access passage to what was originally the family accommodation.* Below: *Three very different types of window at Hanger; from the simple slit to the Tudor double with decorated drip mould.*

Moor Cross House

Moor Cross House was built in the late 1800's, by Lord Blachford for his unmarried sisters, Katherine and Sophia. Later, after leaving Blachford, Lady Georgina resided there.

Between the wars Lt-General Sir Charles Anderson K.C.B., K.V.I.E.,A.M. and Lady Anderson lived there, and Mrs Phyllis Short, née Jackson, remembers working for Lady Anderson: "I left school at thirteen in 1927, and after working for a while for Mrs Luscombe at Wisdome Farm, I went to Moor Cross House as a tweeny maid. There were three maids and I worked my way up to

being a parlour maid by the time I was seventeen. There was also a cook. The General and Lady Anderson had brass finger bowls on the table and they had to be cleaned. We had to whiten the front door of the cooker, and scrub the blue stone floor everyday. General and Lady Anderson had two sons, both married. We didn't go out much, but loved to go down to the river to swim. If we did go out and came back late, we used Mr Stacey's ladder to climb back in without cook knowing. Where we climbed in there were accumulators in the back shed, to provide electric light."

Above left: *Moor Cross House in its early days, late 1800s.* Above right: *The Hunt at Moor Cross 1984.*

The Shepherd-Haynes Family

When my great-grandfather, George Haynes, sailed home from Australia, where he had been prospecting for gold, with no more success than the acquisition of a wooden leg, hinged at the knee, which he made himself, he met and married Harriet, daughter of John and Betsy Shepherd of Tor. The year was 1869; George was 39 and Harriet 21. They lived in the outer cottage at 'Bays', two dwellings converted from barns which originally served Cornwood Farm, situated where the school now stands.

George, an able craftsman, turned his hand to cordwaining (boot-making), his father's profession, and Harriet occupied herself with raising their eleven children; the last of which was my grandfather, Percy, born when his father was 61 and Harriet 43. Percy only knew his father for eleven years; George died leaving Harriet to struggle on with the help of her older sons, who were more like uncles to my grandfather.

Harriet was remembered by her grandchildren as a sweet-tempered and kind old lady. She died in 1930 at the age of 82. Of the eleven children, the oldest boy, William, followed his father and grandfather into the bootmaking business, and built himself a workshop from a small donkey-shed in the middle of the village (now known as the 'Village Store').

One boy went to London and became a policeman; one emigrated to Canada and was subsequently killed in the First World War. The others all married and lived at varying distances from Cornwood, excepting George and Percy, who

George and Harriet Haynes, date unknown.

stayed on in the village; George working as groom to the Blachford Estate horses.

The 'Haynes boys' were avid duck and hen enthusiasts and frequently won prizes at the village Show. George eventually went into farming, living at Combe Farm for some time, and finally

John and Betsy Shepherd of Tor.

retiring to Cedar Cot (now Broomball House) at Gypsy Corner, on the road to Wisdome Mill. This little wooden cottage had been built by a Plymouth man as a retreat from the bombing of World War Two.

Percy, after being badly gassed in the First World War returned to Cornwood and married

Percy and Beatrice Haynes with their son George at the cottage in Bond Street.

William Haynes, bootmaker.

Beatie James, daughter of the Slade gamekeeper, who lived at Frog Cottage. They resided for a while in a cottage in Bond Street (now named Rose Cottage) but later moved to the inner cottage at Bays, next to Percy's mother. For several years Percy worked as the village postman, delivering letters, on foot, in all weathers, to all the outlying farms as well as the village.

I imagine from this that he acquired his nick-name, Posey (Posty?) Haynes. When this job ended he became a smallholder and market-gardener. The two fields above Bays would be cut for hay every year and various villagers would turn up to help. As a child the whole procedure seemed to me very exciting; watching for rabbits, building the rick with pitch-forks, and anticipating the tea, when all the work was done. There would be mountains of everything topped by freshly scalded cream, produced by my grandmother. I loved to watch her skim the cream off the milk (like a thick Whitney blanket) after it had simmered over a bubbling copper of water in the lean-to outside the back door.

My grandfather also grew flowers which he raised from seed carefully collected the Autumn before, and sold them via the Munford family, who had a Saturday stall in Plymouth Market. On a Friday evening the lean-to would be full of tin baths and buckets of water in which would stand bunch-on-bunch of flowers.

The door at Bays had a huge key; it was unlocked in the morning and stood open all day, no matter the weather. The open door symbolised 'open house'. As I recall, people came and went as if it were a Reuters Office. My grandfather always had time for a 'yarn' and my grandmother always had the 'pot boiling'.

In the Autumn it was time to pick the apple trees. The orchard filled the space between School Lane and Blachford Close, Bays and Fore Street. Windfalls would be put in a tin bath and left at the gate for the schoolchildren to take, but of course, it was always more fun for the boys to climb the orchard gate (opposite the school gate) and 'scrump' one or two on the pretext of 'getting their ball back'.

In my childhood traffic was rare in Cornwood and the boys regularly played football in School Lane at break times. After school we would often go to the bake house to buy half-a-dozen of Vivian's 'tufts' (still ranked as the best bread rolls I've tasted).

The Vivians also ran the village post office. A red phone box stood outside and was well used as very few people had phones in those days. The post-office was also a telephone-exchange. A member of the Vivian family manned the exchange at all times, taking messages for all those with no phone of their own. They sat through the night in a tiny, low armchair, awaiting the infrequent ring needing a connection or the bit of good or sad news needing delivery.

My grandfather had one of the first cars in Cornwood. We often drove in it to Hall Cross and from there on to Hanger Down for a picnic, meet-

Picnic on Hanger Down. Percy Haynes sitting on the running board. Beatie standing in the middle.

ing up with members of the family living at Harford. My grandmother would light a fire and boil a kettle on a trivet. The frequency of the picnics was such that the trivet was always left on top of a hedge on the Down. I suppose it is there to this day, if I only knew where to look!

Cornwood was a safe and enjoyable place to play in, 45 years ago. We built dens on top of the hedges in the lane above the school, chased around the Bays fields being 'cowboys and Indians', and dipped for minnows in the river at Langham Bridge, after having scrambled down the hedge and bank and discarded our sandals under the dry arch.

I also spent some hours at Bridge Farm, with Blanche and Minnie Luscombe (Blanche Andrew and Minnie Kingdom). I 'helped' feed the hens and ducks, collect the eggs, and search for litters of kittens in the lofts above the stables, creeping stealthily around old 'Lion' who was wont to kick.

My grandfather was taught by Mr Septimus Green, who now rests, in his chosen spot, beneath a tree near the church porch.

Pat den Hollander - 1996.

Other Cornwood Families

In common with most rural communities, in the age before the railway and car, families tended to stay in and around one area. Alongside the grand families of note who inhabited the estates such as Slade and Delamore, lived humbler families who formed the fabric of the community. Not only did they provide all the essentials of living, from baking, cordwaining and smithying, they also held the skills and knowledge of natural life around which the country year and community life revolved. These families are still in residence today, and though they may now be scattered worldwide, their names are very much part of the history of the parish: Bowden, Stephens, Shepherd, Haynes, Crimp, Greep, Chamberlain, Cox, Kingwell, Matthews and Skelley.

The photographs that follow are a reminder of the importance of these families in the history of Cornwood parish.

Houndle Cottage, 1923 (destroyed by fire 1942-3). Frank and Esther Bowden lived here when they got married. The man in the road is William Stephens; Muriel Stephens stands inside the wall and next to it. Esther Bowden is holding her baby grandson, Basil Stephens. The lady nearest to the house is Alice Stephens.

Above left: *Muriel and Harry Stephens, with their son Basil on his pony.*

Above: *Slade Mill Cottages where William and Alice Stephens and their family lived.*

Left: *1, 2 and 3 Bond Street. No 3 was the home of Harry and Muriel Stephens.*

Above: *The Stephens family taken at Slade Mill Cottages, c. 1920. From left - back row: Bill (who had the saddler's shop in Cornwood Square); Stan (agricultural engineer and blacksmith at Moor Cross); Jim (farmed at Higher Hele); Alf (in the navy); Ern (lived at Bays); Sid (Blachford carpenter); Front row: Harry (worked at Lee Moor clayworks); Lucy (married Thompson, ran shop in Cornwood); William and Alice (Basil Stephens' paternal grandparents); Eva (married and moved to Plympton St Maurice).*

Above left: *The Crimp Family outside their home at what is now called 1 Vicarage Bridge Cottages, about 1912. From left: Miss Laura Crimp (George Crimp's sister); Mrs Emily Greep; Ida Griffiths, (neice of Mrs Crimp); Mrs Mary Crimp (first wife of George Crimp, groom at Blachford). The lady on the right was a governess at Blachford.*

Left: *Bridge Cottages (built 1898), early 1900s with Mrs Yelland (Gerald Skelley's Gran) in the right-hand doorway and Mary Crimp on the left.*

The Chamberlain Family. G.T. Chamberlain, far right, was gardener at Blachford for 37 years. They lived at Garden Cottage (then known as Blachford Gardens). Above right: Gwen Chamberlain in 1917.

Above left: *Mr Robert Henry Skelley with his wife Rosina (née Horton) and their daughter Emily Rosina in the early 1900s. Mr Skelley also had three sons David William Henry, Robert Fred, and Harry. Mr Skelley laid one of the foundation stones at Lutton Congregational Church.*

Above right: *David William Skelley and his wife, Alice Maude, with their daughter Phyllis and son Clifford. They also had a son David Robert, known as Bob, and a daughter Frances. Alice, née Sercombe had been a teacher at Lee Moor. She died in 1951.*

David Skelley and his family lived at Berry Farm, Lutton, which he ran as a smallholding, milking cows, and with fields scattered around the village, some of his own and some rented from the Yonge Charity.

His grand-daughter, Rosalind, remembers spending many a summer day on Headon Moor cutting ferns (bracken), to dry for bedding for the cows in the winter months.

Mr Skelley also worked for the local council on road maintainance, and part-time for E.C.C. at Lee Moor, transporting stone to Lutton with a horse and cart for road making. He was also a parish councillor for 42 years.

His daughter Phyllis, ran the Lutton Post Office at her home at 3 Gills Cottages, Lutton.

Clifford was in the Home Guard during the war. His son Bob was born in 1919. On leaving school he served an apprenticeship as a builder with his uncle Fred, helping to build two of the houses at Longfield, and 1 and 3 Southview, among others. He then spent some time working at Headon Clay works before joining the army. After the war he returned to the farm, taking it over in 1962.

Far left: *Harriet Daisy Kingwell (1894-1996) was born in Ivybridge, the eldest of a large family. Her childhood was happy and Daisy often recounted that when she went into service her brothers and sisters waited for her in 'Daisy's Lane', near Dinnaton to see what little presents she had brought for them. On her marriage Daisy lived in Cornwood where she was to remain for the rest of her life.*

Left: *Daisy Kingwell Cross, named to commemorate her 100th birthday, stands at the junction of Zeth Hill Lane and the Lee Mill to Cornwood Road.*

Wyn Jones and Nigel Matthews recall the life of Bill Matthews, the Man of the Moor:

"Bill came from South Brent to work at Blachford before the last war. He soon became part of the village with his membership of the Men's Club and his involvement with the football team. As a member of the Parish Council he made clear his concern for the village which he had taken to his heart, as the villagers took Bill to theirs.

An interest of Bill's was motorbike dirt track racing, and he often made the trip over to Princetown, and other places, to watch the events. But his greatest love was the moor and he spent much of his time tramping and camping, and he got to know the moor like 'the back of his hand'. He was not alone on these occasions, for he had his collie dogs - no one is quite sure how many - but five would be a good guess. These dogs were well trained by Bill and it is said that he could round up sheep on the moor, set one dog to watch over them whilst he went off for a couple of hours to round up strays, and then return to find the guard dog sitting just where he had been left.

After the war sheep played an important part in the economics of the parish, as most farms had a flock and dogs to control them - no ATVs then! Early in the 1970s Bill, along with similar minded people, laid the foundations for Cornwood's first Sheep Dog Trials, and these were very successful, with dogs coming from all over Devon and Cornwall. But as the pattern of farming moved

Bill Matthews and friends in the Square.

from sheep to cattle, support for the trials subsided and they are no longer held in Cornwood. The only link with those days is the Bill Matthews Memorial Cup which is competed for at the Cornwood Show each year.

As the years went by Bill could be found sitting on the seat in the Square putting the world to rights with his friends. He died in 1985, missed by many, but not forgotten."

Far left: *John Cox outside Church House, 1938.*

Left: *Elizabeth Cox often helped when babies were born or on the death of a villager. Here she is with her grandchildren Ann and Howard German, outside Church House in 1949. Carbide lighting for the church was stored in the cellar, and it smelled!*

Above: *Ruby Cox, 1936.*

Annie (sitting) and Margaret Cox in 1918. They lived at Church House and Margaret worked at Higher Hele Farm.

Above: *A tunic button of the Air Raid Precautions Service and an arm patch of the Women's Voluntary Service (Civil Defence).* Left: *The commemorative scroll recording the war service of Frank Hayes. Born at Bays, School Lane, in 1884, he emigrated to Canada serving with the Canadian Infantry until his death in 1917.*

Doris Sowden served in the NAAFI in England and then in Italy and Algiers EFI during the Second World War.

Lewis 'Curly' Sowden served in the REME in two World Wars.

War Years

1914 - 1918

In October 1910 it was reported that "Twenty ladies have come forward to join the Red Cross Society in Cornwood, and First Aid lectures are in course of management, at a fee of 2 shillings per head. This is not much for us to give to enable us to tend to wounded soldiers should a war break out in our own country. One object is to organise a small band of men and women who would help in this village, each doing his, or her, appointed work."

No one living in the village today has memories of the First World War. Records of Parish Council meetings show concern with arrears of allotment rent and the introduction of poultry and pigs and the maintenance of footpaths. These mundane entries hide the terrible effect of the war. "Mr. W. Skelly has given up his allotment to take a job as a munitions worker" is one of the few entries directly referring to the conflict.

In 1919 a Faculty Petition was made for the War Memorial. The twenty-seven names engraved on the war memorial bear a woeful testimony to the extent of sacrifice made by our village. The fathers of some living in the parish today were engaged in the conflict, they preferred not to talk about their experiences.

1939-1945

Slowly over the months leading up to the outbreak of the Second World War the peaceful pattern of life in the village changed. In February Air Raid Wardens were appointed in Lutton and Cornwood. In June the vicar, The Revd. Gardner McTaggart arranged first aid classes and reported to the Parish Council that: "in the case of an air raid the children would be rushed off to the back lane which would be covered with iron and a layer of earth on top". Arrangements were made for delivery of lorry loads of sand to the two villages. In August Col. Butler explained the evacuation scheme, he was pleased with Cornwood who offered to take 100 children including 20 for Lutton. A committee of ladies was formed to look at houses and deal with evacuees and the vicar reported that respirators would arrive in due course.

Many recall hearing Neville Chamberlain's announcement of the declaration of war on the wireless at the morning service on Sunday 3 September, 1939. Olive Jeffery (née Sowden) the head housemaid at Blachford remembers young Cyril Passy rushing into the room calling "the balloon's gone up". Cyril became a fighter pilot and was awarded the Distinguished Flying Cross.

Clothing ration coupons.

The use of Ration Books and Identity Cards became routine with life on a strict war footing. The Lutton Co-op store was an important element in the life of the village. Ration Books were held in the shop and stamped with indelible ink when goods were issued. The shop sold clothes, coal, ironmongery and bicycles apart from groceries

Fund raising event on Delamore Lawns in 1941. From left - back row: *Mrs Lawley (wife of the Cornwood School Headmaster). Children: 1. Valerie Phillips; 2. Eleanor Greep; 3. Monica Small; 4. Enid Nicholson; 5. Arny Liddicote; 6. Jill Payne, 7. Margaret Skelley; 8. Dorothy Pryce.* Front row: *1. Arthur Pryce; 2. David Tucker; 3. Lawson Parker; 6. Alfie Mudge; 7. Tommy Squires.*

which were parcelled up and delivered to various households. The Co-op manager L.S.Youlden was a respected man in the community and became Chairman of the Parish Council. When Olive Sowden was married the wedding cake was ordered from the Co-op. A few days before the wedding Mr Youlden told Olive that the cake had been destroyed in an air raid on Plymouth. Somehow, and just in time, a replacement cake arrived from East Devon. It had chocolate icing as there was no white icing sugar.

Blanche Andrew remembers: "The blackout made life difficult for all, windows were covered with heavy curtains and one had to take care when opening outside doors. Lighting and cooking was by paraffin lamps, some cooked on coal or wood fuelled ranges. There was no electricity in Cornwood, however there was a supply to Lutton."

The Parish Council was concerned with the perennial problems of footpaths and increasingly the renting of allotments, the government's encouragement to 'Dig for Victory' was taken very seriously. Stirrup pumps were allotted, one for Cornwood and one for Lutton and training sessions arranged. Extra pumps were available from the Plympton RDC at £1 each. Two hundred ear plugs were issued to Cornwood. Much time on the council was given to organising fund raising

FROM CORNWOOD TO LONDON

Evacuee school children from London to Cornwood who are now returning home. Among their country treasures is a box of silkworms.

A newspaper report of the 1940s recording the return to London of evacuee schoolchildren from Cornwood. The dark-haired girl with the hair-slide is Eileen Hewitt, the girl who later returned to Cornwood and married Harry Willcocks.

campaigns for many important wartime causes including the Spitfire Fund (£100), Aid to Russia, Warship Week (£2,600 HMS *Harrier* adopted), Wings for Victory (£6,000), War Savings, Aid to China and Salute the Soldier.

Bert Small recalls: "200 evacuees with their teachers arrived from Acton in September 1939. They were badly dressed and in poor physical condition compared with village children. When they settled-in their appearance and behaviour improved. The Public Hall was their classroom.

As air raids on London became less severe some returned home. Others were visited by their parents and lasting friendships were established. One schoolgirl, Eileen Hewitt, later returned to the village and became Mrs Harry Willcocks".

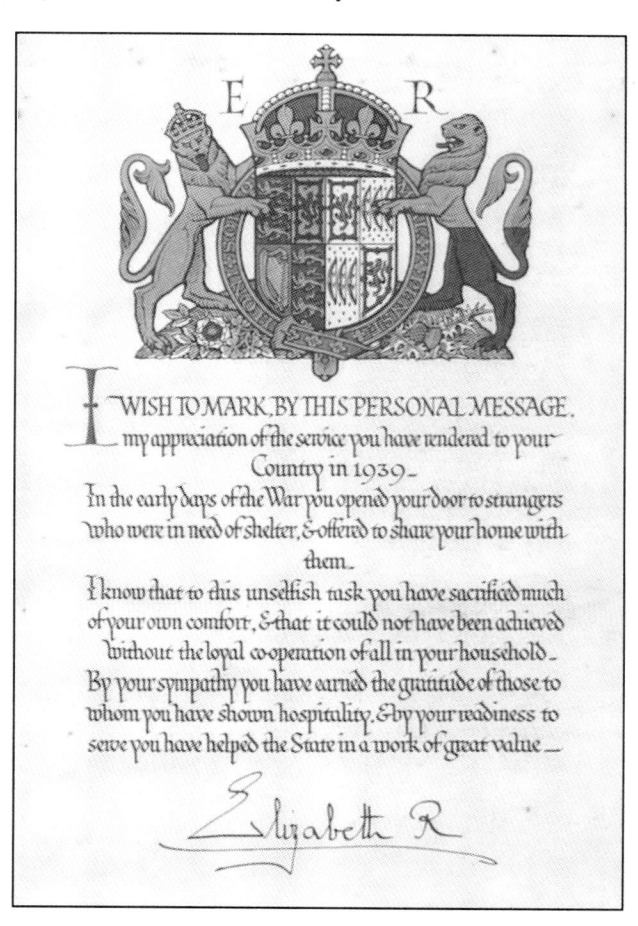

Above: *Dorothy Cox and Edna at 19 Newtown with evacuees, Violet, George and Florrie.*
Right: *A message from the Queen thanking those who took in evacuees.*

The parish provided dormitory accommodation for many people coming out from Plymouth to get a good night's sleep away from air raids. Among them was Frederick Harvey a noted singer, who stayed at No 3 Newtown with Fred Small, and sang in the Public Hall. The film star Robert Newton also appeared on the stage. Scenes from the film 'I live in Grosvenor Square' with Anna Neagle and the American star Jagger Dean were shot at Cornwood station. Mr. Wingate and Charlie Winsor who worked at the station appeared in the film.

Most of those who worked on farms or in the clay pits were in reserved occupations and not available for call-up for the armed forces. Many of them, both men and women, served in the auxiliary services and volunteer organisations such as the Local Defence Volunteers - renamed Home Guard in 1940, Special Constabulary, Fire Service, Civil Defence, Womens Land Army, WVS and other worthy bodies.

There were three Home Guard units in Cornwood, an infantry platoon, commanded by Ernest Broome (he was Col. Parker's chauffeur and lived in Delamore stables). Among those serving were: John Andrew, Frank Broome (son of Ernest), Lewis Mumford, Ned Osbourne, Horace Pearn, Charlie Roberts, Frank Skelley, Thomas Weston and Charlie Winsor. They manned trenches in Mountain Wood to cover tank traps at Alms House bridge and mounted guard on Cornwood station and viaduct. Combined exercises were held with the Sparkwell detachment, one side wearing soft hats and the other tin hats. Sam

Phillips was a dispatch rider on a motor bike. Poles were erected on Hanger Down to deter gliders from landing.

The duty of the Mounted Home Guard was to patrol the moors and report any unusual activity. Among those serving on horseback were Reg German, Bill Greep, Ernest Hext, Harry Hext (Sergeant), Admiral Mackworth (Corporal), and Bill Matthews. Live-firing practice was carried out on the moor and caused problems with nervous horses shying. One horse bolted at the first shot and disappeared into the moor for several days. An altercation between one of the NCOs and a Trooper concerning the suitability of a horse was settled by a reluctant shaking of hands before an officer in Plympton. The Mounted Troop engaged in an exercise with the foot Home Guard at Stone and threw potatoes at the 'enemy'!

Cornwood Special Constabulary, 1944. From left: 1. Reg Champ (of Delmore Gardens); 2. Ernest Baker (game keeper, lived at Delamore Lodge); 3. Jack Thompson (shopkeeper, Bond Street); 4. Bert Kerslake (farmer, Bond Street); 5. Thornton Whitford (clay worker, lived Clergy Cottages); 6. Fernley Cox (clay worker, lived Newtown); 7. Richard Vivian (baker and postmaster, Fore Street); 8. John Glover (farmer, Delamore Farm).

Special Constable Fernley J. Cox, August 1940.

Douglas Drew, on Home Guard duty, August 1940.

Cornwood Home Guard at Delamore Stables, 1940. From left - back row: *2. Thomas Weston (served in army in France & Belgium, 1916-1919, died 1984 aged 101); 3. Charlie Winsor; 6. Frank Skelley.* Middle row: *4. Harry Williams; 7. Charlie Roberts; 8. Lewis Mumford.* Front row: *1. Frank Broome (son of Ernest); 5. Ernest Broome (Col Parker's chauffeur lived at Delamore Stables); Also in photo are John Andrew and Horace Pearn.*

The mounted Home Guard behind Hanger Farm, 1944. Mounted-left to right: *Reg German; Admiral Mackworth; George Ryder; Sgt Harry Hext; Bill Greep (on Mischief); Bill Matthews; Ernest Hext (on Blackbird, who died aged 32).* Standing at front: *Lt Ernest Broome.*

A Clandestine unit 'Churchill's Guerilla Underground Force' was formed - it consisted of seven men. The idea was that in the event of an invasion they would remain concealed in an underground bunker on Hanger Down and emerge after the enemy had passed over to inflict as much damage as possible. Among those from Cornwood and Lutton serving in the unit were Captain Falcon, the Officer Commanding, he lived at Slade, Clifford Andrew, John Andrew, Steve Hosken, Clifford Widely and Andrew Wotton.

To this day those who served in this unit are reluctant to talk about it. After the unit was disbanded Elsie Cannon, the Moyseys and Robert Wotton remember that a digger was about to dig out the pond at Slade when Andrew Wotton suddenly appeared and shouted 'Stop!'. Captain Falcon had arranged for all the surplus ammunition and explosives to be dumped there!

Auxiliary Territorial Units (Churchill's Guerilla Underground Force) consisted of seven men from each village; Cornwood, Diptford, Fleet, Harford, Plympton, Ugborough, and Yealmpton. The Cornwood men are: Third row back: 1. Steve Hosken, 6. Captain Falcon. Second row back: John Andrews; Front row: 2. Clifford Andrews; 3. Clifford Woodley. The photograph c. 1940 was taken at Slade, Captain Falcon's home.

Women At War

Members of the Women's Land Army in their cord breeches, green stockings and pullovers were a familiar sight around the parish. They lived and worked on the farms. Joyce Rendle (née Cane) at 18 years of age was already working at Dinnaton for George Willcocks when the Land Army was formed, she served for four and a half years. Nancy Hare visited farms in the area where Land Girls worked to make sure their living conditions were satisfactory. A number of other women from the parish, although not in the Land Army undertook forestry work.

Joyce Rendle (née Cane) recalls life at the time: "I was already living and working at Dinnaton Farm, for Mr Willcocks, when I joined the Land Army during the war. Every day I had to get up at 6am, summer or winter, and go out into the fields to bring in the cows for milking. They had to be tied in their places ready for the men to come in and milk them, and after the milking I would turn them out again. After that I could go for a fried breakfast, which consisted of fat and lean bacon, fried bread, potatoes and eggs, of course. Breakfast finished, the shippens had to be cleaned

out and made ready for the afternoon milking, giving them some hay and cake in the winter, and also bedding, and later I had to wash out all the milking gear.

In the summer there was hoeing, or scuffling, or hay making and saving the corn - very different from these days. In the Autumn I always had to

Joyce Cane in her Land Army uniform. The photograph was taken in Exeter following a parade of Land Girls. The picture at the top of the page is part of the uniform showing the diamond-shaped insignia each half of which signified 6 month's duty.

pick the apples from three orchards, climbing up the tall ladders, and falling off some times! And most of the year there were vegetables to get for shops in Plymouth - cutting cabbage, kale greens and turnip tops in all weathers. When it was very wet I used to wear thick West of England sacks over my shoulders, and around my waist to help to keep me dry.

During the winter when I cut the kale, I would take it out to the fields in a wagon with a big cart-horse. A few times when I went to shut the gate from the kale field, the horse would start trotting down the road, and I had to run and catch it before it went too far, which was not always before the right gate.

Once in the summer after hay making we were bringing all the gear down to another part of the farm, some of us with the horse and wagon, and some riding the other horses bareback. My horse wanted to get in front and I couldn't stop him, and off I came, head first over his head. I was in a bit of a mess, and my arms and legs got terrible gravel rash. This was about eleven in the evening, as we had double summer time through the war.

When it was potato digging time the farmer's wife used to bring out lovely hot pasties for dinner, to save us from going all the way home. Mr Willcocks also had another farm a few miles away, where we had to dig potatoes and pull mangolds and turnips. The hay and corn harvest and threshing had to be done on both farms. The farmer and his wife were always very good to me, although there was always plenty of hard work. wet or fine.

I stayed in the Land Army for four and a half years, which was the longest time for any Land Girl. We all had a uniform to wear for which we had to give up most of our clothing coupons. Each half year we had a half-diamond shape to sew on our armband which we always had to wear whenever we went out."

Beside the Land Army, women were called upon to serve in other occupations on the land. Forestry workers were known as 'Lumber Jills' and Doris Baskerville recalls her experiences: "During the war all women under twenty-one had to do war work.. Some were drafted to the dockyard, but I refused and was sent to do forestry work. It was hard work outdoors but enjoyable, and the pay was good compared with domestic work. We felled 'dipped' trees and cut them into lengths ready for loading on to lorries.

The trees were sawn into logs at ground level, often in muddy conditions. It needed good technique and teamwork, and the results were used as pit-props. Many of the local woods we see now, such as the Piall Wood area, were cleared at this time.

The foremen were Mr Furber who was from 'up-country' and Mr Whitford who lived in Fore Street. Arnold Luscombe, Bill Darton, Trowbridge Sercombe and Tom Green 'dipped' trees (cutting a notch in the trunk to determine the direction of fall) while Stan Sharman and Wilf Sharman worked as lorry draymen, driving the lorries loaded with timber."

Wartime forestry workers. From left - back row: *1. Rose Gammon (née Osborne, Frank's sister); 2. May Roberts (from Lee Moor); 3. Mrs Griffin (Plymouth evacuee); 4. Beryl Locke; 5. Phyllis Herdman (Plymouth evacuee); 6. Audrey Roberts; 7. Doris Baskerville (née McNeil); 8. Gladys Beable.* Front row: *1. Millie Roberts; 2. ?; 3. ?; 8. Norah Blackshaw.*

Other Wartime Experiences

Although not a prime target area, 37 high explosive bombs, 700 incendiary bombs and 3 unexploded anti aircraft shells fell on the parish, resulting in slight damage to buildings and two sheep killed.

A Stirling heavy bomber returning from a raid crashed when it hit trees on Headon near the top of Gibb Hill opposite the two cottages. The mixed nationality crew were killed. The Home Guard was called out, and later the RAF cleared the wreckage and carved a cross on a tree.

A Blenheim medium bomber crash landed in Five Acres Field off Rook Lane on the lower side of the present Show Ground.

In 1938-1940 a searchlight detachment was established at Watercombe and later moved to Yeo where Royal Marines were stationed. Bert Small tells how early in the war Indian troops with

Royal Artillery searchlight battery at Watercombe, 1939-40. 'Kami' Bill Sykes, 'Cowboy' Jackie' Greenwood, 'Chucks' Jack Comley, Fred Johnson, Bill and Jack with friends.

German POW, Karl Betz, in Cornwood.

mules were stationed in Cornwood. In the Spring of 1943 American soldiers arrived and set up camps at Blachford and Delamore. Blanche Andrew, Elsie Cannon and others remember that there were black and white GI's who were allowed out on alternate days and attended dances in the Public Hall. A lot of the girls made friends with the Americans as they could get silk stockings. Gateways were widened to take army vehicles and a large pond was excavated near Bridge Farm to practice beach landing and waterproofing. The road from Moor Cross to the village was closed, and everyone had to go up through Corntown. The Americans had plenty of food, electricity was laid on to work potato-peeling machines in the camps and was connected to Bridge Farm and the Kerslake's cottage (now Rowan Cottage). In May 1944 General Bernard Montgomery inspected the army units on Hanger Down. Towards the end of the month troops were confined to camp and early in June the camps were deserted. It is probable that soldiers from Cornwood were among the 3000 GI's who died on Omaha Beach in the invasion of France.

The Polish Navy occupied part of Slade and Delamore and buildings around the village. A workshop was established in the Square at the smithy. The Poles had an office at Moor Cross. Blanche Andrew remembers "they were very smart men, and big with it, but much more reserved than the Americans."

The camps were later used to accommodate German prisoners of war who worked on farms and in the claypits and are remembered as being well behaved. Some of them made slippers out of hessian, one gave the Luscombe family at Bridge Farm a painted wooden puppet he had made, and it is still with the family.

Cornwood men were prisoners in Germany. Michael Farr saw much action before being taken prisoner, after escaping twice he was thrown into Colditz and eventually freed by the Americans in 1945. Anthony Parker was captured early in the war. He was a man large in stature and helped in the construction of escape tunnels by pulling up bags of spoil from the excavations although he was too big to go through the tunnel himself.

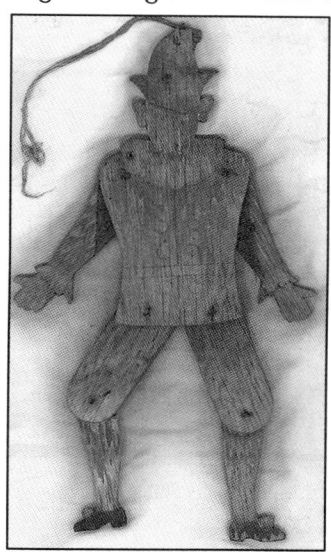

Wooden puppet made by a German POW.

Ann Baldacchino, née Riley, recalls: "During the war I stayed for a time at Delamore where my aunt, Sylvia Oliver, was Colonel Parker's nurse. Colonel Parker invited my mother and me to come and stay at Delamore to get away from the bombing in Plymouth. We stayed with him on the first floor of the house. Upstairs in the attics were some families of Polish refugees and the ground floor was let to some Polish forces people.

We must have been there during the build-up to D-Day, because I remember the field being absolutely full of army tents and soldiers. My mother told me that it was so dramatic because after weeks of there being hundreds of people about all the time, suddenly, silently, one night everyone was gone.

One day while waiting for the bus to take me into Plymouth for school, we saw an American soldier by a hedge with something in his arms. It was a young rabbit and he asked us to look after it for him. As we had a rabbit hutch we said we would, and asked him the rabbit's name. He said 'Damastus' - I don't know if that would be his first or surname, but anyhow, we called the rabbit 'D-Day Damastus' - a long name for a little creature!"

Ann Riley with her aunt Sylvia Oliver and 'D-Day Damastus'.

Barbara Simpson also remembers the war years: "For the first two years of the war I worked as a nursing-auxilliary in Plympton First Aid Post (Air Raid Precautions) and our mobile van was used to go around the villages with a doctor and staff giving anti-diphtheria injections. We came twice to Cornwood, (on the 8 February and on the 26 March 1942) when on the last occasion, I have it noted in my diary, we immunised 83 people. Dr Brown of Plympton was the attending doctor."

Ray Tremeer's wartime memories are equally as vivid: "My grandparents, Felix and Lois Tremeer, lived at Stone Farm, Cornwood, and at the outbreak of the First World War in 1914 Felix rejoined the Navy - his name, together with that of his youngest son Arthur, is recorded on the memorial in the village church to those killed in the two World Wars. Lois, my grandmother, came from another Cornwood family, the Colliers. My father, Felix John Tremeer, lived most of his life in Cornwood and died in 1989. There are several members of the Tremeer and Collier families buried in the churchyard.

I was born in Cornwood in 1931 and spent my first 21 years there. Most of my wartime recollections revolve around Hanger. In 1939 our evacuee, Leonard, arrived, and I remember my first question to him was "How old are you?" When he said "Eight", I replied "Oh good, so am I!"

The Cornwood evacuees were all from Acton. They brought their own teachers with them and their school was the Village Hall. When the Plymouth Blitz started (much earlier than the heavy bombing of London), many evacuee parents decided that Cornwood was not very safe after all, and gradually the evacuees returned home. However, while he was with us, Leonard introduced me to a new game - it was called 'Playing Truant'! The evacuees also introduced the village children to comics - most of us had not seen these before, and our eyes were opened as we read the *Beano, Dandy, Radio Fun* etc.

Hanger Down during the war was protected from enemy aircraft landing by hundreds of telephone poles, which looked very strange. From Hanger we had a grandstand view of the Plymouth air raids. The skies were lit up with searchlights, tracer bullets, flares, anti-aircraft tracers and the huge fires burning in the city. The noise was incredible, and to a young boy quite exciting. Then one day my mother took me into Plymouth soon after a bad raid, and I saw for the first time the sickening destruction caused by the bombs. I never again thought the air raids were exciting.

One winter evening, as the bombing started there was near panic as people rushed to get out of Plymouth. My sister and I had been taken to the city by my aunt, and as we tried to board the bus for home a young man jostled my six-year-old sister and pushed her off the platform. This so incensed my Aunt Mildred that she flayed about him with her umbrella until justice was done and Diana was safely aboard.

As the anti-aircraft defence of Plymouth improved, more and more enemy bombs were jettisoned in and around Cornwood. I remember vividly one night when the bombs came very close to Hanger, and the whole family, including my old grandmother, huddled under the big pine kitchen table. The next day we gazed at the huge

Ray and Diana Tremeer in the orchard at Hanger Cottage, about 1938.

craters caused by the high explosive bombs, in the fields around us. Everywhere there were jagged bits of shrapnel which we boys collected. Later in the war we collected the pieces of silver paper which the Germans dropped in an attempt to foil our Radar.

I used to travel to Plympton Grammar School by train each day on the 8.30am from Cornwood, returning on the 4.30pm from Plympton. One evening I missed the train home, and that very day was the occasion when a German plane buzzed and strafed the train as it slowly crawled up Hemerdon incline. No damage was done, but I was sorely 'miffed' to have missed the excitement.

Plympton Grammar School was severely damaged by two high explosive bombs in about 1942. We boys thought the school would be closed for months, so extensive was the damage. But within a few weeks it was all repaired and we were back at school. Right through the war however bleak the situation, the education of children was given top priority. I remember with affection and gratitude many of the old retired teachers who came back to the classroom to replace the younger teachers who had been called-up.

We really knew that the war was going our way when the American troops arrived in about 1944.

I was amazed on returning home from school one day to see my first bulldozer - it was enormous, and it was being driven by a Black GI (another first for me) to level the site of a huge American base in the grounds of Blachford - it extended right up to Moor Cross. We got to know quite a few of the GI's - some as young as 18 - and occasionally they would have tea with us on the wall of Hanger Lane. Later we learned that many of these young Americans were killed in the D-Day landings.

Eventually the war ended, and there was great rejoicing. I inscribed some details of the event on a piece of slate and placed it in a granite wall at Hanger. I wonder if it is still there? However, rationing of food continued, and now included bread (not rationed during the war) so that supplies of wheat could be diverted to Germany.

Two of my Cornwood cousins joined the Royal Air Force during the war. Cyril Phillips was killed over Germany in 1942, aged 19. Jack Bradley, whose escapades are described elsewhere in the book, baled out of a stricken Flying Fortress in 1945 when he was 19, and became a prisoner of war. My uncle Arthur Tremeer who joined the Duke of Wellington's Regiment, was killed at Nuymegen right at the end of the war.

During the war all the church bells were silenced, but could be rung in an emergency such as the expected enemy invasion. The first daylight anti-aircraft fire over Cornwood caused smoke-rings - which were mistaken for German parachutes, causing the church bells to be rung. This story might be apocryphal, but it was widely told in the village, for years afterwards, with much hilarity."

Hanger Cottage in 1936, home of the Tremeer family. Three years later it was to be seriously damaged in a fire that started in the thatch and quickly spread to the adjoining cottage to cause a blaze that could be seen for miles around. Mr Tremeer had to battle through smoke to rescue his daughter Diana from her bedroom.

Blanche Andrew, who lived at Bridge Farm Cornwood, also remembers the arrival of the American troops: "The black Americans came to Blachford Lawns and got everything ready before the white Americans arrived. There were tents all over Blachford Lawns with nice slabs making paths to each tent.

They had electricity to work the potato machines. They did all their cooking at Blachford - masses of food with no shortage. We had some tame lambs and the Americans used to make a fuss of them. Once the lambs were all sticky as they had found one of the big tins of jam that the Americans had, and they liked it.

The Americans made a great massive concrete slipway into the river in the field next to Bridge Farm, and they used to drive their vehicles into the water for testing.

In a shed at the other end of the meadow they stored hundreds of cans of petrol. They had to make the gateways to the fields bigger so that their vehicles could get in. When we told them that their tanks were too big, they said 'Our tanks aren't too big, its your roads and gateways that are too small.'

When the Americans had gone there were German prisoners of war on Top Lawn, the other side of Puttapool. They went to help on the farms. One of the Germans made a puppet and gave it to my mother, Mrs Ruby Luscombe (see page 137). They didn't have much to eat.

On the 29 December 1943 there was a fire at Bridge Farm. It was at night and we were all asleep. Minnie was a light sleeper, and she thought she heard the horse, Duke, who had itchy feet against the gate that was galvanised along the bottom. She heard crackling and pulled back the heavy blackout, which was velvet, and saw the courtyard was one glow.

Bridge Farm, Cornwood, before the fire of 1943 which destroyed it.

We had no phone and I had to go to Mr Stacey who rang up the Fire Brigade. Looking back I could see flames going up. Mr Sandover, landlord of the Cornwood Inn, was the chief warden, and he brought some spirits to treat the inhabitants. The fire hydrant wasn't deep enough to take water.

Mr Lawley was at the School House and Minnie and I went there to sleep. We only had what we could grab as we left. The cellar and the granary were still intact and then Major Passy built the bungalow. They never knew what started the fire, though some thought it could have been a boy stealing oil."

One of the heroes of Cornwood during the war was Jack Bradley. As the *South Devon Times* of 1 December 1944 reported:

'The Distinguished Flying Medal has been awarded to Flight-Sergeant Norman J Bradley. RAFVR. in recognition of numerous operations against the enemy, in which he has invariably displayed the utmost fortitude, courage and devotion to duty'.

As a boy Norman James Bradley lived at 18 Newtown in Cornwood. His friends at Cornwood School knew him as Jack, as his grandfather didn't like the name Norman and always called him Jack, so the name stuck. In May 1942, at the age of seventeen and a half years, he joined the RAFVR, and trained as a gunner. He completed thirty-two operations over enemy territory, and then became a gunnery instructor. He was later recalled to flying duties, and posted to 214 Squadron, which was engaged on special duties.

On the night of 14-15th March. 1945, Jack was in a group of seven men captured near Baden-Baden, after parachuting from their damaged RAF B17 Flying Fortress bomber. They were taken by civilian police to the little village of Huchenfeld. where, in front of a jeering crowd, five of the group were executed as spies by members of the Hitler Youth. Jack and another crew member, Tom Tate, ran for their lives and managed miraculously to escape. They were later recaptured by the German army and imprisoned, but survived to give evidence against the executions at a war crimes trial after the war.

In the summer of 1995, the *Western Morning News* printed an appeal by Tom Tate for any knowledge of the whereabouts of Jack Bradley. Edna German, who knew Jack Bradley at school, saw this and contacted Jack's cousin, so setting the wheels in motion for an unforgettable re-union after 50 years.

In July 1996 Jack Bradley and his son visited Huchenfeld. There is now a plaque in the village to commemorate those men who had died.

Above left: *Jack Bradley, known as Brad, rear gunner with 166 Bomber Squadron, Kirmington, June 1944.* Right: *With the crew of a Lancaster at Kirmington, June 1944. Pilot John Boles, a New Zealander is in the cockpit.* From left: *John 'Dickie' Dickinson, John Hughes, Jack Bradley, Jim Seaman, Tony Madden and Arthur Harding. The design on the side of the aircraft is 'Tiki', a Maori good luck charm.*

Those who worked and lived in the parish through the war years were proud of their relations and friends who served in the armed forces around the world. Their loyalty and achievements brought great credit to the villages. So many took up arms that it is not possible to single out individuals in this brief account, some were wounded and sadly the following names were added to those on the memorial who gave their lives in the First World War:

A.P.L. Armstrong
J.I. Gordon
A.A. Ham
L.L. James
R.G.K. Knowling
P.J McCarthy
T.D.R. Parker
I.H.D. Passy
C. W. Phillips
W.T. Sandover
E.H. Shepherd
A.G. Tremeer

The news of the Allied victories in Europe 'VE Day' on 8.May 1945, and over the Japanese 'VJ Day' on 14 .August was greeted with joy and relief. Flags and bunting appeared in the streets and adorned the houses. Dances were held in the Public Hall and a tea party was held for the children. The schoolmaster, Mr.Channing conducted a Service of Thanksgiving in the parish church as the Vicar was not well enough to attend.

Although the atmosphere was of celebration and happiness, many experienced moments of stillness as they recalled the frightful experience of total war endured by everyone.

Rationing of food and clothing continued, as time passed villagers adapted to a new way of life with the realisation that things would never be quite the same.

Norah Blackshaw recalls post-war life in 1949: "The war was over and all young Service Couples wanted to set up homes so Utility Furniture was introduced. In order to get this one had to apply for Dockets or Units. We had enough Units to buy a wardrobe, a dressing table, a bed, three piece suite, dining table, sideboard and three chairs. After paying cash, the firm refused let us have even one more chair. In order to get this chair I had to enter the Black Market, as it was called in those days.

My young brother-in-law was in the army, stationed in Italy, so I wrote and asked him to try and get another pair of Pure Silk Stockings, like the ones he had sent me - gold dust in those days!

This he did, by putting one in a letter to me and the other in a letter to his Mum. By then I had the offer of heaps of units in exchange for the stockings, but I only wanted one chair!

We moved all our furniture and belongings into a two-roomed flat in a big country house, 7/6 a week rent, where we lived happily for eleven years, and during that time we saw twenty-one families move in and out."

The Falklands War

The Falklands War of the early 1980s, was the last conflict in which Britain independently went to war against another nation. Short and sharp in duration, it is remarkable that so small a parish as Cornwood should provide no fewer than six men who served with the Task Force.

Those who returned were treated as heroes throughout the country, and the people of Cornwood were equally determined to show their thanks for those who had returned safely to their homes and community.

Thus, in August 1982, following a victorious campaign, the Cornwood Inn became the scene of celebrations and presentations, including a telegram of thanks from the Governor and people of the Falkland Islands.

The welcome home celebration at the Cornwood Inn for the members of the Falklands Task Force, August 1982. From left: Captain P.L. Bancroft RM; Colour Sergeant T. Morrison RM; Lieutenant P. Schular RN; Major E. Southby-Tailyour RM; Pte Brian Worrall, 3 Para; Pte Graham Worrall 3 Para.

The Canberra, *which served as a troop carrier and hospital ship, bringing Task Force members back into Southampton in 1982.*

Getting Together

Whether you kick a ball, tread the boards, bang a drum, hit leather with willow, make jam, camp, research, walk, march or ride, you will make friends by enjoying yourself with like minded people. A lively village will always have a great deal of activity going on and Cornwood and Lutton are no exception. Some of the clubs and activities have left little trace, and perhaps they did not last long. The *Cornwood and Lutton Magazine* has always been a vital means of communication for all manner of activities, and the following entries give some idea of the variety of interests that local people have.

April 1965

The Young Women's Social Club is mentioned. They celebrated their second birthday in 1966. It was an open club for single or married women of any denomination which met in the vicarage every Monday evening. Mrs Edith Hamley was its president, and one of its activities was to help provide refreshments, entertainment, parties and outings for the Friendship Club.

September 1965

The proposed Cornwood and Lutton Bowling Club were to use the vicarage tennis court.

In May 1975 an advertisement appeared, seemingly aimed at the local 'Devon Dumplings'.

> *"WAIT" FOR IT! Ladies. The Battle of the Bulge is being fought on Fridays, 2.30-3.30pm (during school term only) at Cornwood Public Hall. Everyone welcome, whatever your shape, to our keep fit sessions accompanied by Mrs Babb on the piano. A small charge is made to cover the cost of the hall. Tea and biscuits are NOT served during the interval.*

As far as we are aware no results were published!

In February 1 1978 Geoff Cook started Lutton Joggers. Feeling lonely on the road, he was pleased that about half-a-dozen people joined him on two or three evenings a week. They enjoyed each other's company for a year or two. A table tennis club was to start in September 1 1989 and it ran for at least one season. A local History Group also began in the 1980s, and one of the tasks they undertook was to record interviews with the older villagers so that their memories of village life were not lost.

In the following pages are recorded a number of the activities that make, or have made in the past, Cornwood parish such a vibrant community.

Cornwood Brass Band

The Cornwood brass band, with two clarinetists, in the early years of this century.

As in many westcountry villages, the brass band was an important part of community life, as *Cornwood Parish Magazine* reported.

September 1893
Harvest Festival, September 27th. 272 guests sat down at tables for a repast enlivened by the strains of the Cornwood Brass Band, which also provided music for the 116 dancers who enjoyed themselves in the school at the close of the day.

November 1894
The Cornwood Brass Band, which was established many years ago by Lord Blachford, and has been a credit to the parish, besides affording beneficial recreation to a number of young men, *has rather fallen off of late, but an earnest endeavour is now being made to put new life into it. A fresh instructor, J E Crompton, Bandmaster of the Devonport Borough Band, an excellent teacher and a fine cornet player, has been engaged to teach once a week for the next two months, and then fortnightly.*

May 1895
On May 10th 1895 a concert was held, which was highly successful, musically, numerically and financially, realising £4.2s.4d (net) for the funds of the band, which is making good progress under the instruction of Mr Crompton.

The date of disbandment is not known.

The band on the Heathfield. It was established by Lord Blachford at some time before 1893, meeting on Monday and Wednesday evenings. Mr and Mrs Fry of Corntown appear to have been leading members. An annual engagement was to lead the villagers from the Square to Cornwood Show ground 'playing mightily all the way'.

The Royal British Legion

The 16 January 1997 marked the fiftieth anniversary of the formation of the British Legion, Cornwood Branch, at a meeting chaired by Col. W. Passy at the Library, Lutton, on that day in 1947. Before that British Legion members in Cornwood had belonged to, and had helped run, the Sparkwell Branch. Branch Officers and a General Committee, which included two ladies, were elected, whilst a Branch Standard was ordered a few weeks later and was consecrated at church and chapel services in June 1947.

For forty of these years Tom Squires has been Branch Standard Bearer. In that time he has paraded the Cornwood Standard at the Festival of Remembrance at the Royal Albert Hall in November 1981, and at the R.B.L National Annual Conference in Plymouth in 1995.

By 1948 membership totalled 97, plus 11 honorary members. In November 1948 a Women's Section was formed, and the Women's Section Standard was dedicated at the Parish Church and the Congregational Chapel on 20 February 1949. The first Women's Standard Bearer was Mrs M. Warley.

One of their first social functions was a Garden Fete held at Delamore on 17th August 1949, and which over 300 people attended. And throughout the 40 years of its existence (it disbanded in 1988) this, one of the smallest Women's Sections in Devon, carried out invaluable work in supporting the ex-service, old age, and youth communities of Cornwood and Lutton.

The Lutton Library became the Legion Hall, and with both sections now in being full programmes of social and fund-raising events were held at the Legion Hall and elsewhere. This fund-raising was in aid of the primary function of the Legion - assisting and supporting ex-servicemen and women, and their dependants, and perpetuating the memory of those who died in the service of their country. 'Service, not Self' has always been the watchword for Branch activities.

Handing over the British Legion Standard following consecration in 1947. 1. Bert Rider (of Shaugh Prior); 2. Col. W. Passy; 3. William Phillips; 4. Alfy Kingwell; 5. Percy Mudge; 6. Harry Willcocks; 7. Norman Willcocks; 8. Leonard Drew; 9. Clifford Cox; 10. Joe Haynes; 11. Edwin Luscombe; 12. William (Taff) Skelly; 13. Percy Luscombe; 14. Mr Gubb; 15. Pat McCarthy; 16. Harold Friendship; 17. Herbert Sharp; 18. Peggy Downing; 19. Rev N. Nesbitt; 20. Richard Willcocks; 21. Mrs Noel Passy.

British Legion party for old folks at Cornwood, 1954. The South Devon Times *reported: 'On Saturday about 40 old age pensioners and widows sat down to high tea at the Legion Hall, Lutton, Cornwood, as guests of the committee and members of the Ladies Section of Cornwood Branch of the British Legion. Funds had been raised by a succession of whist drives and competitions. Tea was followed by community singing, games, dancing and vocal items. A vote of thanks was accorded the committee and helpers on the motion of Mrs Eva Prout, one of the senior members of the Ladies Section.* From left - back row (standing): *1. Dick Drew; 2. Mrs Em Wilcox; 3. Mrs Burge; 4. Miss Allen (evacuee); 5. Mrs Luscombe; 6. Mr Luscombe; 7. Mrs Adams; (co-op bread); 8. Mrs Nora Jenkins; 9. Mrs Julia Nicholson.* Middle row (sitting): *1. Tom Prout; 2. Dick Phillips; 3. Mrs Hard; 4. Daisy Mudge.* Front row (sitting): *1. Elsie Willcocks; 2. Mrs Sinclair; 3. Mrs Tapper; 4. Mrs Eva Prout; 5. Mrs Pope; 6. Jack Blackshaw; 7. Sarah Blackshaw.*

Cornwood Cricket Club

There have been several cricket clubs. In April 1905 the parish magazine reported a problem familiar to all organisations: "We are sorry that Mr Endocott's engagements compel him to resign the secretaryship of the Cricket Club, on which there is a balance in hand of 8s 3d. We hope the club will start again in good time."

In, July 1910 it brought the good news: "We have at last started a Cricket Club amongst the young men of the Parish. No village the size of Cornwood should be without a Cricket Club. It lets off the superfluous energy which is so liable to find vent in objectional ways, and teaches men to 'play the game' in life." (written by the Vicar, Rev. J F Powning).

Nothing more is known until autumn 1953, when B. Horton and Mr Blackshaw asked Major F.A.V. Parker of Delamore to support the formation of a cricket club. A public meeting was held and the decision to go ahead taken. Funds were raised by holding dances, and the *South Devon*

Times reported on 19 March 1954: "The newly-formed Cornwood Cricket Club held their first dance at Delamore, home of the chairman, Major F A V Parker. About 330 guests danced to Frank Fuge's orchestra. Equipment was bought. Major Parker made Oak Park available for a pitch, and the wicket was cut by his mower. The first match was played in May 1954 by a team who were all Cornwood parish men. The changing room was an old battery shed and a galvanised shed was erected by members in which the ladies provided tea for the teams for 9d.

In March 1982 *Cornwood and Lutton Magazine* reported a small ceremony in which a red oak, the Cannon Oak, was planted at Oak Park in memory of Dennis Cannon, a farmer and former chairman of the Parish Council. It should eventually provide shade for generations of spectators. In 1990 a Colts Team was started. It has been successful in encouraging young cricketers ever since. In 1997 the club is a thriving organisation.

Early sports photography. Cricket on the lawn at Delamore, 4 October 1910.

The first Cornwood cricket team following the reformation of the club in 1954. From left - back row: 1. Bill Blackshaw; 2. Powell; 3. Jack Blackshaw; 4. John Whitford; 5. Roger 'Maxie' Marshall. Front row: 1. Lawson Parker; 2. Bill Horton; 3. Les Hurn; 4. Major Parker; 5. Garfield Baskerville; 6. Ern 'Tubby' Baker; 7. Tonkin.

The Friendship Club

In September 1964 Maud Roberts, Ida Willcocks, Dorothy Barker, Barbara Olver, Phil Hambly (the vicar's wife), Ruth Colton and Barbara Drew (now Mrs Green) met to discuss the formation of one of the most consistently popular clubs in the village. The club's first funds were sixpence from each lady: a total of three shillings and sixpence! Mrs. Green reports that: "Various fund raising activities continued and in January 1965 an open meeting was held in the British Legion Hall, Lutton, to see what support there was. It was very well attended and after much discussion it was decided to have our first meeting in February 1965 and that it would be called the Friendship Club."

Cornwood and Lutton Magazine was able to report that the meeting was a great success with over 30 people attending. It was decided to hold meetings in the British Legion Hall on the third Tuesday of the month. This birthday is celebrated every year with a party. As some members found it difficult to attend in inclement February weather, after some years the party was moved to the April meeting. From October 1972 to March 1973, meetings were held at Delamore. After that they moved to their present venue, the Sunday School at Lutton. Members enjoy playing cards and bingo, followed by tea, for which a small charge is made. There are about 50 members, although there were as many as 72 at one time. The club is run by a committee of seven, who used to refer to themselves affectionately as 'the girls'.

Members pay a small annual subscription and raise additional funds by draws, coffee mornings, bring-and-buy stalls and whist drives. The result of all that effort is that the committee is able to organise two or three summer coach trips, birthday and Christmas parties (with invited guests), all of which are free!

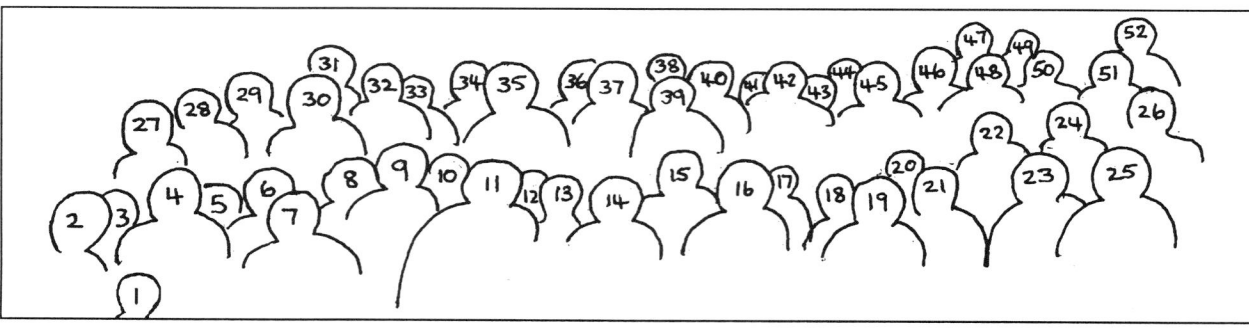

Cornwood and Lutton Friendship Club Birthday Party, 1977. 1. Marion Blackshaw; 2. Ellen Sharman; 3. Gwen Clemo; 4. Mr Chris Nicholson; 5. Eileen Willcocks; 6. Brenda Reed; 7. Mr Pamell; 8. Phyllis Kingwell; 9. Alf Kingwell; 10. Pat McNeil; 11. Emma Willcocks; 13. Mrs Whitford; 14. Julia Nicholson; 15. Charlie Willcocks; 16. Barbara Devine; 17. Mrs Smith; 18. Ida Skidmore; 19. Ida Willcocks; 20. Rene Lillicrap; 21. Ethel Skelley; 22. Joyce Nicholson; 23. Mrs Sampson; 24. Norah Blackshaw; 25. Mrs Vanstone; 26. Ruth Colton; 27. Barbara Drew; 28. Blanche Andrew; 29. Fernley Willcocks; 30. Wyn Jonas; 31. Barbara Olver; 32. William Jonas; 33. John Andrew; 35. Mrs Wreford; 36. Gwen Tall; 37. Mrs Greep; 39. Mrs F Willcocks; 40 Mrs Wakeham; 42. Miss Horton; 43. Emmie Sercombe; 45. Mrs Phillips; 46. Mrs Nicholson; 47. Valerie Badger; 48. Olive Wilcox; 50. Laura Sowden; 51. Miss Happle; 52. Mr Greep.

Cornwood Amateur Football Club

An early Cornwood football team. The players are: Mayhew, Eric Roberts, B. Blackler, Alf Rendle, C. Yelland, I. Kelly, C. Rendle, Turpin, C. Bastard.

Cornwood AFC has a history of disbanding and reforming since its inception back in 1900, the 1900/1901 season being the earliest that can be found in the *Western Evening Herald*, when the club was in the second division of the Devon County Football Association.

Success and failure have naturally been part of its chequered past but for most part, it has been an enjoyable cornerstone of village activity with players generally happy to participate, whatever the result. When the club was originally formed, and for the first half of the century, there was always a good stock of hearty local working lads to ensure a good selection to make up a regular winning team. These men, more often than not, would be clay workers or farm workers living and working around the village.

The Second World War was a turning point for Devon and Cornwall, as men from all over the UK were stationed in Plymouth, either as servicemen or dockyard workers. As a purely local team, this also marked the turning point for Cornwood Football Club, with outsiders moving in. Bernard Lawrence, who played for Cornwood after the war recalls: "Cornwood was a thriving community when I signed on in 1946, after being demobbed and the team was well respected - and feared! I remember in 1950 we were drawn against the mighty Newton Abbot Spurs for the semi-final of the Devon Senior Cup. We played magnificently against this semi-professional side and were holding them to a 1-1 draw when they were awarded a penalty just as the final whistle was due. They scored of course, which put them through to the final - which they also won.

Dave Barker, a local lad and regular player for Cornwood in the early 1950s remembers, as a teenager, watching Charlie Fields, a talented footballer who had moved down from London and who had signed on for the club in the 1947/48 season. In the first game of the season and in his first for Cornwood, against Ermington, Charlie scored 9 goals in the first half, at the end of which he allowed himself to be substituted. I think we still won the game, 9-1!

Whilst the influx of outside talent has had a positive effect on the prowess of the team, there have been less and fewer locals in the squad, with a consequence that village support for the team has gradually subsided. Nevertheless, enthusiastic team members, either locals or outsiders have always managed to whip up local support and the Cornwood Inn has always endeavoured to oblige. One particular memory is of Cornwood winning a cup tie at home and being rewarded by Alan Coulthwaite, owner of the Inn in the early to late 1980s, bringing up a barrel of beer, a barrel of lager and all the glasses to Heathfield in the back of his estate car, to celebrate winning through to the next round.

The club has always had its own pitch at Heathfield, adjacent to the main entrance to Delamore, where one of its most famous patrons, Major F. A. V. Parker and his family resided. The changing hut on the northern side of the pitch still stands today, probably as long as 70 years after it was first built.

So, here we are in 1997 with nearly 100 years of Cornwood football history behind us.

Cornwood football team 1900-1901. Centre back: Mr William Harvey. From left: 1. Mr Reglar; 2. Mr Henry Glover; 3. Mr Blackler; 4. Richard Luscombe; 7. Mr Rendle; 8. Mr Jackman; 9. Mr Pascal. Sitting: 1. Arthur Skelley; 4. Andrew Newson; 5. Mr Skelley. Other players during the season were J. Roberts, T. Chapple, S. Worth, R. Hillson, F. Legg, R. Mumford, T. Triscott and M. Elliott.

Cornwood AFC Combination Cup winners 1947-48. From left - back row: 1. Harry Bennett; 2. Charlie Fields;. 3. Reg Skidmore; 4. Bernie Moon; 5. Ern Tricky. Middle row: 1. Pip Aldridge; 2. Alistair Roberts; 3. George Greenland; Front row: 1. Bernard Lawrence; 2. Jack Blackshaw; 3. Ernest Waddup.

Cornwood Football Team, 1950-51. From left - back row: 1. B. Lawrence; 2. R Skidmore; 3. A Roberts; 4. Jack Blackshaw; 5. ? George Greenland; 6. W Waddup. Front row: 1. P Aldridge; 2. C Fields; 3. A Kerslake; 4. A Neil; 5. L Trickey.

Cornwood AFC, 1983-4. From left - back row: 1. Harvey Thomas (Manager); 2. Ian Cooper; 3. Kingsley Ward; 4. Ian Kerslake; 5. Mark Frearson; 6. Ivor ?; 7. Ian 'Moff' Moffatt; 8. Gary Davies; 9. Steve Jones. Front row: 1. Howard Johnson; 2. Mike Perry; 3. Roy Roach; 4. Paul Sterland; 5. Martin Wills; 6. Alan Wills.

Cornwood Guides and Brownies

It is not known when Cornwood Guides were started, but a newspaper report places it earlier than 1922. In 1932 *Cornwood and Lutton Magazine* mentioned that the Lieutenants were M. Stacey and P. Sandover. The Brownie Captain was M. Passy. The meetings were held in the Guide Hut on the Heathfield. The *South Devon Times* carried the following report in April 1955:

FLYING UP

The First Cornwood Girl Guides and Brownies had an evening's entertainment in the Guide Hut on March 16th. *The programme commenced with a "flying up" ceremony when four Golden Hand Brownies "flew up" to the Guide Company. The Guides acted in two plays "Jumble" and "The Pie and the Tart".*
The Brownies sang two gypsy songs dressed in traditional costumes and played singing games. A new Brownie was enrolled by Mrs Box, the District Commissioner. The programme ended with a camp fire sing song.

The Cornwood Guide Company closed in 1966 and became the Sparkwell Company.

Far left: *Cornwood Brownies 1922. Ida Griffths stands at the far right with Betty Shepherd kneeling at the right.*

Left: *'Tick' Tall and Betty Harvey of 1st Ivybridge Girl Guides camping at Blachford, 1930. Mrs Passy was the District Commissioner.*

Cornwood Girl Guides, 1962. From left - back row: *1. Jennifer Skidmore; 2. Lorraine Pringle; 3. Andrea Greep; 4. Pam Sherrin; 5. ?; 6. Janet Poynter; 7. Lesley Mudge; 8. Lesley Channing; 9. Jennifer Thorrington; 10. Yvonne Nelder; 11. Margaret Blackshaw.* Middle row: *1. Jennifer Greep; 2. Mrs Doris Wills (Brown Owl); 3. Mrs Box; 4. Mrs J. E. Eastleigh (County Commissioner); 5. Sister Betts; 6. Mrs Phyllis Channing; 7. Hilary Channing; 8. Shirley Downing.* Front row: *1. Jean Devine; 2. Carol Weaver; 3. Kay Phillips.*

Cornwood Cubs and Scouts

The first evidence of a Boy Scout troop in Cornwood comes from a photograph taken at Delamore in 1912.

Nine boys of the troop attended the Imperial Rally of Scouts at Birmingham in 1913. The Scout Jamboree at Mount Edgcumbe in 1934 was also attended by a good number of Cornwood and Lutton Scouts.

Over the years the strength of the pack has fluctuated and has been disbanded and reformed a number of times. In 1978 a new Cub Pack was formed with D. Butler as Akela and Group Scout Leader Mr den Hollander. In July 1996 the Cub section went to the 'Cuboree' in Wadebridge, Cornwall which 2000 boys and girls attended under Acting Leader Pam Keane. Great Stert provided the venue for the 1st Cornwood Scouts Camp Fire and Barbecue to which, in August 1996, up to two-hundred people attended. It was held to raise funds to upgrade some camping equipment and it did. Cornwood Scouts, Cubs and Beavers are flourishing!

Contrasting styles in Scouting. Left: *c. 1910, Bill Roberts who lived at Berry.* Right: *1977, Donald Brown.* Above: *Sam Dobinson, 1997, Beaver of the Year Award.*

Scouts camping at Cornwood, 1932. From left-back row: *Ken Roberts; Alistair Roberts;* Middle row: *Arthur Stephens; Clifford Cox;* Front row: *not known.*

Tucking into breakfast at the Wadebridge Cuboree in 1996.

Cornwood Women's Institute

In 1917 the world was at war; women did not have a vote, but in Cornwood women voted to start a branch of the Women's Institute.

Cornwood W.I. was one of the first hundred to be formed, on 20 June 1917, and it was only the second W.I. in Devon. The W.I. was formed under the Agricultural Organisation Society as can be seen from the membership card of Mrs. D.E. Drew, below, a founder member of Cornwood W.I.

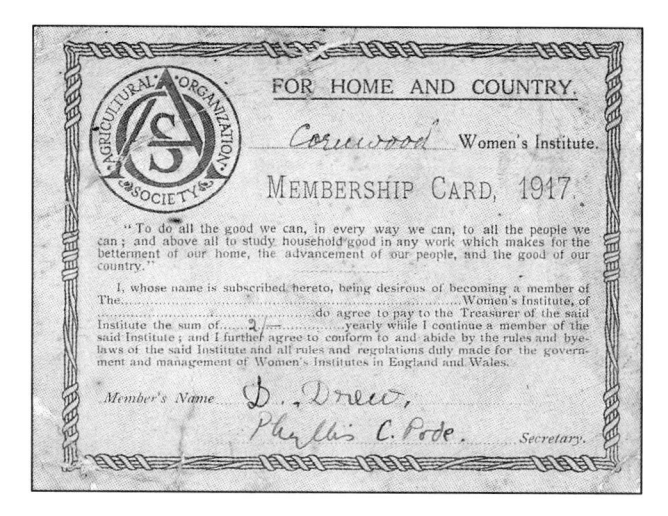

In 1918 Cornwood W.I. ladies were organising themselves to help the war effort. It was proposed that a Pig Club be started, also keeping of geese and goats on Cornwood Common, and names were taken of those willing to start a livestock club. On behalf of the Ministry of Munitions, members collected fruit stones and nut shells which were used to neutralise poisonous gas.

Muriel Bloomfield recalls joining Cornwood W.I. in 1927: "The meetings were held at Delamore House; the lady of the house, Mrs. Parker, was our President. Meetings were well attended, which showed real commitment when one thinks of the distance from the villages. Most members came on foot and there were no street lights to help. Few people had transport.

Our next venue was at The Guide Hut, situated on Heathfield. We were there until the hut was burned down. For many years our membership was near, and at times exceeded, 100. The numbers have gradually decreased over the years as women became involved with other interests and other organisations came into being."

Now nearly eighty years on, the WI. meet in the Public Hall and a W. I. representative sits on the Hall Committee, which is discussing proposals for a new Public Hall.

Muriel Bloomfield says that "attitudes have changed over the years. One instance being that for many years the President was always a lady from one of the Manor Houses, therefore a certain amount of class distinction had a place in our

WI Production of Henry VIII, Glebe House, April 1936. From left- back row: *1. Dolly Locke; 2. Betty Shepherd; 3. May Shepherd; 4. Frances Olver; 5. Alice Hillson; 6. Olive Wilcox; 8. Kate Stancombe; 9. Frances Bowden; 10. Margaret McNeil; 11. Mrs Riches; 12. Mrs Shepherd; 13. Mrs Stephens; 14. Joan Thompson; 15. Blanche Luscombe; 16. Joan Rendle; 17. Mrs Rendle.* Front row: *1. Mrs Passy (Henry VIII) 2. Maggie Roberts; 3. Mrs Roberts; 4. May Poynter; 5. Margaret Nicholson; 6. Muriel Roberts; 7. Esther Bowden; 8. Olive Sowden.* Round the table: *1. Mrs Kit Stephens; 2. Laura Sowden; 4. Minnie Luscombe. With the exception of Henry's all the costumes were made by the members of the cast and backroom girls.*

lives." In 1930 members agreed that girls could be admitted to Cornwood W.I. at the age of fourteen.

As the W.I. is an educational charity, speakers have always been the major part of the monthly meeting - in 1918 a speaker was invited on votes for women; in 1926 it was 'Modern Miracles' as the speaker termed the rapid strides made in the care of different diseases. In November 1928 the speaker gave what is described as a most interesting lecture on 'The Romance of a Shopping Basket'!

Some things have stood the test of time, the annual hyacinth bulb show in 1925 had 43 members entering and this is still held each year, although on a much smaller scale.

Muriel Bloomfield says: "There has always been great interest in amateur theatricals, ranging from short humorous sketches suitable for the 'social evenings' which were a part of village life. In 1936, we won a shield there for presenting the Trial Scene from King Henry VIII."

The 80th Anniversary in 1997 was the first celebration without any surviving founder members. Following a thanksgiving service at the church, members and guests travelled to The Glebe for the Anniversary Garden Party.

In eighty years, members of Cornwood W.I. have enriched the lives of their fellow members through the fun and enjoyment of learning at the monthly meetings.

They have contributed to the life of the parish by planting trees, roses, daffodils at various locations; entertained and provided refreshments. They have made their voice known nationally by attending the National Annual General Meeting where resolutions which affect the population generally are discussed.

Most importantly, for eighty years they have upheld the object of the W.I. which is "to enable countrywomen to take an effective part in the improvement and development of the conditions of rural life".

Celebrating the Golden Jubilee of Cornwood WI at the Glebe, June 1967. From left - front row: *1. Elsie Wotton; 2. Phyllis Phillips; 3. Rachel Mudge; 4. Ethel Sandover (cutting cake); 5. Cis Mumford; 6. Mrs Stephens; 7. Nell Stephens; 8. Gwen Andrews; 9. Daisy Kingwell; 10. Mrs Blackler; 11. Mrs Thomson.* Behind: *Blanche Andrew; Barbara Drew.*

Celebrations

Do we need an excuse to get together and enjoy ourselves? In Cornwood and Lutton whether there is a national or local reason or not, the people have, over generations, provided entertainment and enjoyment for themselves and others, and a good time has been had by all.

The 1912 September edition of the Cornwood Parish Magazine discussed various Church matters, but also gave the first clue to the date of the Cornwood Show's origin by referring to it as the sixteenth of such. The 'wretched weather affected the attendance' unlike that of 1996 when glorious sunshine was enjoyed and the crowds gathered. Perhaps the modern custom of the secretary running around the field wielding an onion on a stick at first light guarantees the fine day so essential on the occasion.

The first reference to the Horticultural classes is as early as 1905. "The beautiful weather favoured the annual show of the Cornwood Cottage Garden Society on July 26th. When the Cottage Garden Society joined with the Horse, Cattle and Sheep sections has not, at present, been possible to ascertain.

But then, as now, the centre of attention was the horticultural tent with "table decorations, etc., making a splendid display" a reference to floral art? There were Butter and Cream classes, a dozen eggs, coloured, won by Miss Andrews, white won by Master Balkwill, and Honey won by F J James. The 1911 magazine lists the horticultural classes of the period; Broad and Runner Beans, Carrots, Parsnips, Tripoli and Spring Onions, Shallots, Round and Kidney Potatoes, Apples, Fruit, Peas, Tomatoes, Cucumbers, Sweet Peas and a vegetable collection.

Major Parker won several classes in the Open Section, in part presumably, as he had at least one gardener to help him. Winners included familiar village names, Phillips. Rendle, Shepherd, Smerdon, Nicholson, Mills, Horton, Blackler and Greep.

The 1911 show was blessed with ideal weather. £34 was taken at the gate. Well we might seem more sophisticated now with Trade Stands, Craft Tent, Children's Sports, Magician, Tug-of-War and Dog Show, as well as three Horse Rings. But whatever the differences, the continuing success of the show reveals that the people of Cornwood and district can enjoy themselves much as their forbears did, and that the place of the village show has not yet to be consigned to history.

Above left: *Mr S. Mudge giving an opening address at the Cornwood Show, 1949.* Above right: *The Cornwood Show celebrated its centenary on 16 August 1997 at East Rooke Farm. Equestrian classes, along with classes for donkeys, cattle, sheep, dogs, pets, flowers and vegetables, were supported by tug o' war, a magician and a clown who entertained a large crowd.*

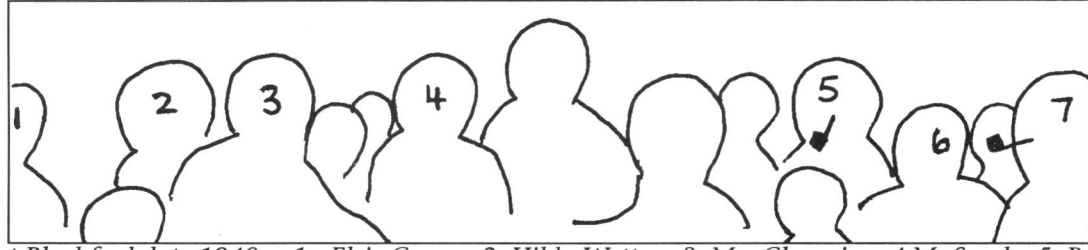

Fete at Blachford, late 1940s. 1. Elsie Canon; 2. Hilda Wotton; 3. Mrs Channing; 4. Mr Smale; 5. Reg Champ (ex-captain of bellringers); 6. Sid Shepherd (from Hall Farm) 7. George Willcocks (from what is now called Coriander Cottage).

A juggler entertains at The Fair in the Square, 1990.

Then and Now

Whether entertaining themselves, or looking after visitors, Cornwood has always made the most of opportunities to celebrate while offering a warm welcome to others.

Top: *In the 1920s outings were made to Cornwood from Plymouth by charabanc. Behind the Cornwood Inn people would set up stalls and serve teas. From left- back row: Chrissie Collins; Annie Steer (Reg Steer's sister); Mrs. W. Sandover (from the Cornwood Inn); Jack Small. Front row: Mrs Tom Newman (known as Granny Newman); Elizabeth Cox; Mrs J. Small; Esther Bowden; Kathy Honey; Ada Newman.*

Below: *80th birthday celebrations of the WI at the Glebe, June 1997. From left- back row: Carol Baker; Rosemary Elsworth; Brenda Roberts; Elizabeth Chetwyn; Wyn Jonas; Visitor; Betty Colton; Margaret Garmston; Ivy James; Frances Rendle; Kath Sergeant; Joyce Rendle; Sheila Brown; Marjorie Hall; Norah Blackshaw; Gill Ryder; Barbara Thomas; Sue Warry; Marjorie Northey. Front row: Janet Northmore; Heather Fraser; Rachel Mudge; Muriel Bloomfield; Pat Hill; Anita Donne; Pam Keane; Doris Pengelly; Blanche Andrew; Meriel Dobinson; Sally Fairman; Frances Rogers; Edith Skelley.*

Subscribers

Subscribers outside Devon are indicated as such in the list

Mr E. S. Werrey-Easterbrook
Mr G. Colton
Mr A. J. Warley
Meriel and Eric Dobinson
Shân Dobinson
Chris and Kim Dobinson
Dr J. Carlson
Mr and Mrs A. Jennians
Mr and Mrs M. Matthews
Mr E. J. Luscombe
Mr Thomas Squires
Mrs J. Skelley
Mr John Goldman
Mr Douglas Richard Drew
Mrs Dorothy M. Thomas
Mrs Olive Jeffery
Barbara S. Thomas
Mrs Marion Blackshaw
Mrs M. Dyer
Mr B. I. Stephens
Mrs Doris Baskerville
Mrs Jean Netherton
Mrs E. Carleton
Margaret Atkins
Mr and Mrs M. J. Hoyle
J. D. Cornish
Mr Alan Hill
Mrs K. M. Stancombe
Kate and David Jones
Mr and Mrs P. G. Francis
R. A. Elsworth
Mrs E. M. Cannon
Mr and Mrs Robert Cannon
Mrs P. Long
Mr and Mrs I. Davenport
Lewis J. Munford
Mr S. E. Beddow
Keith and Mary Davies
Mrs N. G. Jenkins
Gladys Blackler
Mr C. E. Cox
Ivybridge and District Civic Society
Keith and Mrs Judith Farmer
Jonathan C. Farmer
Matthew I. Farmer
Gerard T. Farmer
Mrs J. E. Reed
Mrs T. Melling
Mike Brown
Mr A. Cox
Mr C. Cox
Mr P. Hurn
Mr M. Cox
Peter and Barbara Cook

Mrs Nadia Hitchins
Mrs B. F. Small
South Hams District Council
Paul Rendell
D. S. G. Dollard
Delamore Estate
A. B .C. Dollard
Margaret Bullock
Willie Skelley
Michele Renshaw
Mrs D. Pengelly
R. Baskerville
R. P. and E. M. German
Howard and Sue German
D. R. Wilday
Mrs D. E. Barker
H. Pryce
C. Barker
Mrs C. Harris
Jacquelyn Hoare
Mrs H. Yu
Mrs Margaret A. Tielman-Ward, Suffolk
Dave and Kath Brewer
Mr E. A. and Mrs P. L. Dolman
Mrs E. E. Moysey
Richard Moysey
Wendy Robertson
Patricia Den-Hollander Haynes
Sue Haynes
Jonathan Haynes
Mrs P. Slatter
Mrs B. Roberts
Mrs S. Brown
Mrs S. Bradley
L.M. Dollard
Richard Ivor John Phillips
Miss Sue Warry
Louise Smee
N. J. Bradley
Malcolm Sheryl, Dorset
Mrs C. J. Northmore
Paul Salmon
Mrs Jean P. Hawkins
G. Cook
P. R. Johnson
B. M. Johnson
Mr R. Mudge, Leicestershire
R. H. Sampson
Mr James Frederick Underwood
Mr Stephen James Ham
Mr Robert Oliver Mudge
Mrs B. E. Everett, Hampshire
Mrs Norah Blackshaw
WBB & Co Plc

SUBSCRIBERS

Mrs B. Devine
Mrs M. J. Oram
Dr. R. H. Bruce
Lt-Colonel and Mrs Charles McLaren
Mrs Iris Cox, Hertfordshire
T. Haynes Maddock
Miss Audrey Groom
Mr D. Furber
Jane Burden
Mr Graham F. Baskerville
Mr Ian and Mrs Rita Devine
M. S. Hawkins
Mrs P. Short
Mrs D. Cole, Buckinghamshire
Mrs B. D. Green, East Sussex
Mrs R. A. Andrew
Mrs B. Drew
Dr. Jill Spencer
Mr and Mrs Kenwyn Clapp
Atkins Family
Mrs R. A. Geake
Mr P. M. Bowden
Tony Barber
Sally Fairman
Mrs Norma Roach, NSW, Australia
Mrs Janet Gearon
Mrs M. E. Goodman
Mrs M. Bloomfield
Basil and Marilyn Sharp
Mrs Maureen Hockaday
Rev J. Rose-Casemore
Patricia L Balsdon
Mr D. Hanna and Miss L. Diffey
Mr Roger (Joe) Osborne
Sheila M. Williams
S. G. Harris
Dr A. G. Stevens
J. F. F. Northmore
Dr. Gordon Mudge, Surrey
Mrs Hilary E. Newcombe (née Channing)
Mrs Lesley Harte (née Channing)
S. M. Cousins, Cornwall
Mrs D. E. Matthews
Mrs Rosalind Clark
Mrs Nancy V. Hawkins, Victoria, Australia
Mrs Noel Passy
Mrs Helen Dewis (née Passy)
Mr Harry Passy
P. J. Nicholson
Mr A. Radmore
Mrs C. M. Godfrey
Anthony Hurn
Carol Hingston
Tony Locke
Mrs M. Blake, Mid Glamorgan
Andrew Blake
Mr H. Pryce, London

Brian Mead
K C. Parnell
Freddy Woodward
Jeremy Woodward
Cathy Scales
Rob Woodward
Mr W R S Parnell
Dr and Mrs K. W. J. Bowen, Oxfordshire
Mr T. R. G. Baskerville
Peter Nelder
N. C. Halliday
Mrs W. M. Jonas
Mr P. O'Doherty, Oxfordshire
Brian Le Messurier
Mr George Mackay
Mrs G. Glen-Leary
Donald C. H. McDonald
L. J. Turpin
D. H. M. Northey
Dr C. K. Langley, Hertfordshire
Mary Rendall, Wales
Mr Leslie E. Skidmore, Lancashire
Mrs Mary Skidmore
Mrs Margaret M. Tully
Mr Ivor J. Skidmore
Mr and Mrs Robert and June Cox
Mrs V. M. Wills
Mr A. Phillips
A Sutton
Mr and Mrs D. A. Butler
Mrs Teresa Jane Schambron Gwinup
Mr and Mrs R. Platts
John D. Bewsher
Mrs Handford (nee Crimp)
Mr Sydney Gerald Short
A.J. and C. S. Hutson
Charles F. Hankin
Mrs Barbara Mills
Jacqueline Coggon
Mr M. R. Keane
A. Watson
M. H. Goodall
Dartmoor National Park Authority
Mr D. G. Masters
Katrina and Simon Parkinson (née Stringer)
David and Wendy Stringer
Fiona Cluett
Mrs E. Hambly
Mr Clive F. Smith
Mrs N. K. Van Der Kiste
Jane and Jimmy Crosby, Cheshire
Mrs J. Butcher
Gary Nicholson
Verna Harder, Kansas, USA
Peter Yolland, Kent
Mrs P Fraser

Mr and Mrs Northey
Mr K. E. Hartley
Mrs G. A. Howard
Linda Bennett
Tom Rapson, New Zealand
Sqn-Ldr. D. and Mrs R. Edwards
Jonathan, Helen and Bradley Nicholls
John and Margaret Shinner
Bernard and Anne Nicholls
Liz and Dave Tarr
Hazel Nicholls
P. G. Odling-Smee
R. R. Willis
John and Mary Abbott
Alistair Abbott
Nicholas Abbott
Janie Abbott
Miss J. Lee
Mrs Jenny Sanders
Mr E. W. Luscombe
Mr and Mrs D. W. Puttick
Mr and Mrs K. Owen
Mr P. Hamilton Leggatt BSc.
Mr and Mrs Harris
Mr and Mrs Rolfe
Richard and Oliver Field
Colin C Kilvington
Mr J. H. Reith
Mr G. Waldron
Mr and Mrs A. Cook
Mr and Mrs G. W. S. Gilliam
Mr N. J. Osborne
Rev. C. F. and Mrs S. Small, Glos.
Mr and Mrs Michael Baker
Mr Clifford Skelley
Robert John Couch
Marie Ann Couch
Mrs B. E. Simpson
Charles William Rendle
Eileen Balkwill
Bill and Yvonne Langdon
Gillian Glegg
Mr and Mrs P. S. Sandover
Mr and Mrs Rose
Mrs M. J. Dorey (née Osborne)
Mrs S. K. Owen
Mrs P. Lake, Sussex
June Puttick, Sussex
M R. F. Miller
Mrs Marilyn Small
Mr and Mrs C. Gillespie
Mr and Mrs M Thomas and
  Mrs J. M. Poynter
John Faulks, Essex
George and Sue Gandy
Mr A. Graham
Mr Bryan Locke

Derek Locke
Leslie Roberts
Chris Lloyd
Elisabeth and Tom Greeves
Mr B. Bewsher
Mr and Mrs Gordon Nelder
Chris McIntosh
Miss B. A. Basden
E. F. Coote
Richard and Susan Merritt
Mr Michael John Goodliffe
Mr and Mrs Eric Phillips
Mrs Susan Kerswill
Mr R. F. F. Steer
Mr Garry Worth, Canada
Mrs Sharon Lorz (née Worth)
Mr Clive Willcocks
Mr and Mrs Kerswill
Mr and Mrs D. Warley
Mr K. C. Turpin
Neil and Sarah Hunter
Mr A. Hurn
K. J. Mumford
Sue Pritchard-Jenkins
Cornwood C. of E. Primary School
Jane Hewitt
Mr J. R. Nicholson
Mr and Mrs Luckraft
W. J. Short
Mrs N. K. Thomson
J. P. Bearne
Mrs Karen McLean, Canada
Mr L. A. Cooper
Mrs B. Andrew
Mrs Kingdom
Miss Sarah Perry
Mr P. Symons
K. J. Burrow
Una Hodges (née Ham), Australia
Mrs P N Willis
R. I. Yonge, Surrey
Olive and Ken Walter
Mr B. C. Blight, Cumbria
Mr R. S. Blight
Mr and Mrs P. West
Mr and Mrs Graham Downing
Mr and Mrs Keith Downing
Mrs Edith Skelley
Anna and Simon Butler
Mr R. E. Tremeer
Mr B. R. H. Targett
Linda J. Hungerford, Queensland,
  Australia
Jeanne White, Queensland, Australia
Mr and Mrs David Farnham
Mr Frank Henry Beer
Mr and Mrs J. D. Dennis